Chatham House P

Turkey and the West

Chatham House Papers · 27

Turkey and the West

David Barchard

The Royal Institute of International Affairs

Routledge & Kegan Paul
London, Boston and Henley

The Royal Institute of International Affairs is an unofficial body which promotes the scientific study of international questions and does not express opinions of its own. The opinions expressed in this paper are the responsibility of the author.

First published 1985
by Routledge & Kegan Paul Ltd
14 Leicester Square, London WC2H 7PH
9 Park Street, Boston, Mass. 02108, USA and
Broadway House, Newtown Road,
Henley-on-Thames, Oxon RG9 1EN
Set by Hope Services, Abingdon and
printed in Great Britain by
Billing & Son Ltd, Worcester

ISBN 0-7102-0618-6

Contents

Acknowledgments

This study would not have assumed its present form without the generous assistance of many people. I should like to thank officials of the European Community, members of the Permanent Delegations of Turkey, Greece, the United States and the United Kingdom to the North Atlantic Treaty Organization, and of the British Foreign and Commonwealth Office, for taking the time to discuss with me some of the themes covered in the following pages. Many errors and some inconsistencies were disposed of by those who were kind enough to attend a seminar at Chatham House in January 1985 to discuss the first draft of this paper. Joan Pearce, head of Policy Studies at Chatham House, was an unflaggingly patient and constructive editor. The manuscript benefited from the attention of Susan Walker at several stages. My profoundest thanks go to all those whose conversations with me over a number of years have helped me form my opinions.

May 1985   D.M.B.

1 Introduction

Turkey and the West

Relations between Turkey and the Western world can be expected to alter significantly over the next decade as Turkey consolidates its achievement in building an industrialized and urban society. Turkey is the first Middle Eastern and Islamic country to achieve genuine industrialization within the framework of the nation-state. The cultural and political choices it now faces are less straightforward than they appeared to be in the 1930s. Turkish society is not merely divided about these choices; it is only partially aware of them.

Turkey's long history of involvement in the politics of Europe, and thereby the West, does not offer clear guidance for the future. Primarily because of the religious divide between Christianity and Islam, the history of Turkish-European relations is largely one of confrontation, antagonism and mutual indifference, dislike or misunderstanding. The cultural divide remains strong even today.

Since 1952 Turkey has played a full part in most Western and European international institutions, from NATO to the OECD to the Council of Europe. This involvement has been somewhat procrustean and occasionally controversial. Turkey's army is larger and poorer than most NATO armies. Its social and economic statistics — and requirement for aid — are far from typical of OECD members. Turkey's credentials as a member of the Council of Europe have several times been challenged, and Western diplomats privately admit that Turkish membership of the Council is possible, even in normal circumstances, only if something of an exception is made on various matters of principle.

From the Western point of view, Turkey's geographical position makes it a valued strategic ally. The political and military balance in the

1

Middle East would be hard to imagine if Turkey were overtly neutral or pro-Soviet. Nevertheless, Turks — and their culture — are little known despite their presence in increasing numbers in all Western countries, and there is little press or academic interest in Turkey.

From Turkey's point of view, despite some of the psychological complications and ambiguities which are regularly encountered in late-modernizing societies and which were most freely ventilated in Turkey in the 1960s, when freedom of discussion was at its greatest, involvement with the West would appear to have brought a range of benefits. Contact with advanced industrial societies remains the chief source of innovation and advance in Turkish society. It is also, it seems fair to say, the main source of improvement where liberal values and human rights are concerned. For this reason even left-wing intellectuals in Turkey who argue for an autarkic or isolationist industrial order, aimed at self-sufficiency, tend to value non-economic links with the West. The relative success of Turkish industrialization since 1963 has begun to blunt the force of arguments, characteristic of 'Third World' societies, which claim that Turkey's dealings with the West are a simple pattern of inferiority, penetration and exploitation.

At the political and institutional level, while Turkey's links with the West have been largely taken for granted for three and a half decades, day-to-day relations have been dominated by tensions which have acted as a brake on the development of a very close or warm involvement. Western diplomats in Ankara would no doubt argue that these are reflections of important differences between Turkish and Western societies. Administrative entanglements with bureaucracy, confrontations over human rights issues, the endless round of the media — these form a quite different agenda from that facing the architects of Danish-British or French-Norwegian relations. Crucially, the nature and role of public opinion is different. Is this something that can be expected to change as Turkish society changes?

In practical terms, then, the West's relations with Turkey tend to consist of a set of institutional connections of varying durability upon which different tensions operate. The most stable of Turkey's institutional connections with the West is undoubtedly its membership of NATO — which, though put to a certain amount of hamfisted questioning in the 1978-9 period when a centre-left government was in power, has never seriously been in doubt. The most problematic of Turkey's institutional affiliations is that with the European Community. Unless (as is occasionally argued) the Community is now in effect merely a 'political bloc', EC-Turkey relations involve both sides in momentous choices about their own identity. Other economic links – with the OECD, the World Bank, the International Monetary Fund or the International Finance Corporation – are essentially workaday problems of implementing policy decisions already taken. Other political links (for example Turkish membership of the Council of Europe) are in normal times relegated to the diplomatic stratosphere, far beyond the sight of Western public opinion. But the more Turkey and Turks begin to impinge directly on Western societies, the more important political tensions will become. These can range from affronts to national pride (unfavourable publicity over drugs cases, for example) to the contest between Greece and Turkey. It may not be a simple accident of history that during the past decade the historical antagonisms between Turks and Greeks and Armenians have re-erupted after half a century of relative dormancy to bedevil Western diplomacy in the Eastern Mediterranean. If so, the going may get tougher rather than easier, as East Mediterranean societies become more intertwined with Western and European institutions without economic and social convergence at a more fundamental level.

Without genuine convergence – which in Turkey's case implies both continuing success at industrialization and a clear act of will – Turkish-Western relations may continue to be beset by a litany of minor, but not negligible, diplomatic grievances, frustrations and irritations on both sides. But if one assumes steady development of the Turkish economy to at least the point reached by Spain in the 1980s, skilful emphasis on like-mindedness and practical cooperation could offer the West an enrichment of which it may not be aware: the accession of a large and dynamic society of 65 million people with a distinctive contribution to make – towards the life of Europe in particular and the West in general – by means of its pragmatism, resourcefulness and human spirit. Rejection of the idea of convergence – or failure in the attempt – may be expensive for both sides, and result in a proliferation of the kinds of minor dispute which complicate Turkey's relations with the West and have turned such gatherings as the meetings of the Turkey-EC Joint Association

Council into minor arenas for political elbow-wrestling, to the annoyance of everyone involved. In theory at least, the West's defensive position vis-à-vis the Soviet Union would be weakened. For Turkey, the alternative to a more organic involvement with the West is probably greater isolation, perhaps disguised by a strong bilateral relationship with the USA (though for various reasons this does not seem very probable), or some kind of superficial Islamic or Middle Eastern coloration. There is no real avenue for a thoroughgoing Turkish reintegration with the Middle East, if only because Turkey is not an Arab country, and in any case the scope for integration with its southern neighbours is relatively slight. If Turkey had not firmly signalled its intention to stay outside the Russian and East European world, as it has done for several centuries and most recently by joining NATO, it would be easier to imagine it going in that direction than somehow 'returning' to the Middle East. The basic choice for Turkey seems to be between some form of isolation or, despite the statistical incongruities and mutual uncertainties, a fuller involvement with the West. But until the evolution of a traditional society into a modern and urbanized one falls into a complete perspective, the second option will involve an element of faith.

Some international comparisons

The Turkish media frequently publish comparative statistics illustrating the country's relative backwardness in European terms. These have perhaps become slightly less common in recent years as the perceived economic and social differences between Turkey and other OECD countries have appeared to be narrowing somewhat. Comparisons between Turkey and its Middle Eastern neighbours are seldom made.

The differences between Turkey and Western Europe remain striking and have to be borne in mind when one assesses the future of its relations with the West. However, some of the disparities are being mitigated by time, and some of the available data are more than half a decade old.

Turkey's demographic statistics offer the most striking contrast. Whereas the net annual increase in population in Britain and West Germany is 0.1 per cent, and around 1.0 per cent in Greece, Spain and Portugal, the Turkish population is growing by 2.3 per cent a year. This is despite a very high infant mortality rate in Turkey: 131 per thousand in 1982, as compared with 16 per thousand in Greece, 26 per thousand in Portugal, and around 11.7 in Britain and West Germany. Although, since 1980, approximately half the population of Turkey has lived in towns and the proportion is growing, agriculture is still overwhelmingly preponderant in the structure of employment: 60.2 per cent of Turks work on the land, compared with 28.3 per cent in Portugal, 29.7 per cent in Greece, 18.9 per cent in Spain, 6.0 per cent in West Germany and 2.6 per cent in Britain. Conversely, industry accounts for a much lower proportion of the workforce: only 16.3 per cent, compared with 35.7 per cent in Portugal, 30 per cent in Greece, 36.1 per cent in Spain, and 44.8 per cent and 38.0 per cent in West Germany and Britain respectively. Turkey's notional unemployment figure of around 20 per cent is equally out of line.

Literacy statistics are disputed, but the 1980 census suggests that approximately a third of the population aged eleven or older is still illiterate. In 1980, according to OECD gross figures for full-time secondary school enrolment, only 37 per cent of the relevant age-group in Turkey was registered for full-time education, compared with 55 per cent in Portugual, 81 per cent in Greece, 87 per cent in Spain, 79 per cent in West Germany and 82 per cent in Britain. It has to be noted, however, that the proportion has steadily expanded in recent years (it was during the 1970s that primary education effectively became universal in Turkey), and that Turkey has a larger university student population than Britain.

Health statistics present a similar contrast. The startling disparity in infant mortality already mentioned has long puzzled demographers, since it is well above what is generally expected for a country of Turkey's socio-economic level. Life expectancy, too, is lower: about 54 years for males in Turkey, compared with 65 in Portugal, 70 in Greece, Spain and West Germany, and 68 in Britain. Figures for doctors per thousand of the population are also well below other OECD countries. As for weekly working hours, whereas most of the workforces of the OECD countries work between 37 and 42 hours a week on average, the figure for Turkey is believed to be over 50 hours a week, although the predominantly agricultural character of the workforce makes direct comparisons difficult.

The relative affluence of OECD populations is indicated by the following figures:

	Turkey	Portugal	Greece	Spain	FRG	Britain
Cars per 1,000 inhabitants	14	118	79	178	346	262
TVs per 1,000 inhabitants	75	141	156	252	337	404
Phones per 1,000 inhabitants	39	149	302	329	488	507

(Again it must be pointed out that these figures are based on statistical data from the late 1970s and early 1980s, and that for telephones and televisions, in particular, there is a steady annual increase.)

In 1979, 5,071 books were published in Turkey, compared with 1,472 in Egypt and 2,397 in Israel, 5,726 in Portugal, 4,664 in Greece, 24,569 in Spain, 59,660 in West Germany and 41,864 in Britain.

In general, the statistics make it difficult to compare Turkey either with other Middle Eastern countries or with Western Europe. In contrast with the latter, however, it is not its relative backwardness but the pace of change which seems most important. Turkey is currently still undergoing the combination of rapid population growth, urbanization, industrialization and socio-cultural transformation which most West European countries experienced a hundred years ago, and it looks as if it will not settle down to a stable pattern until the first or second decade of the next century. Unlike the industrializing countries of nineteenth-century Europe — but in common with most of the so-called Third World — it can no longer rely on migration abroad to offset the pressures of population increase. In most sectors (for instance energy), demand is growing faster than supply. The market for consumer goods continues to expand. So, too, does the labour market: nearly half a million people are added to it each year, and it is impossible to provide employment for all of them.

There are also marked variations within Turkey itself. The Istanbul and Marmara region could in many respects bear comparison with other European industrial areas, at least on the Mediterranean. A thousand miles away, in the mountains above Lake Van, the timeless condition of the nomad is only slowly giving way to settled agriculture, and large towns are relatively new arrivals on the scene: a comparison with Europe is virtually meaningless.

Yet Turks judge themselves by the standards of Western Europe, and it is this comparison which has provided the spur for their country's development efforts this century. The gap may be closing, but it remains formidable. In the early 1980s, GDP per capita was $11,360 in the USA, $13,310 in West Germany and $9,340 in Britain. Per capita GDP in Turkey was $1,170 in 1980 (and less in subsequent years as a result of exchange-rate policies), well behind the $2,430 of Portugal, the $5,650 of Spain or the $4,210 of Greece. These figures raise serious questions about the feasibility of an economic union, such as full membership of the EC would imply, with Western Europe, unless the more advanced partners were willing to devote a very large amount of their resources to equalization.

Turkish society and its institutions

Western images of Turkey tend to be static and sometimes anachronistic. For cartoonists, Turks wear fezes — outlawed since 1925. For press photographers, women in veils are used to symbolize the country. Such images can obscure the political and social realities of a country which is increasingly urban and industrial and in which power has rested for almost the entire period since World War I with an upper class whose life-style is both anti-traditionalist and virtually indistinguishable from that of many Western Europeans.

None the less, the persistence of a highly visible strand of traditionalist and Middle Eastern features in Turkey's life is probably the chief reason why the country's European credentials remain open to challenge. The ubiquitous presence of veiled peasant women in big cities (something not found in Greece, Spain or Portugal) is one of several features of Turkish life — the public role of the army, the cult of the founder of the Turkish Republic, the deep hold of religion on rural society — which suggest fundamental differences, possibly incompatibilities, with West European society, at least as far as eventual economic and political integration are concerned. These are sensitive topics in Turkey, seldom, if ever, discussed in public. The response to comments made by foreigners on these points tends to be that the country is merely travelling at a later date along a path of social and cultural evolution already mapped out by other countries of the northern Mediterranean, and that its progress will be accelerated by involvement with European societies and institutions. The older generation of Turks tends to point to the deliberately pro-European orientation of the country's development drive from the 1920s to the 1950s. This ignores the crucial point that during the 1920s and 1930s modern industrial society and Western Europe were largely equated. Since 1960 a variety of factors — decolonization in Asia and Africa, the success of several late-modernizing Far Eastern countries, the oil boom in the Middle East and the relative decline of Europe in its global importance, to name a few — have blunted the force of the idea of pursuing an exclusively European identity as a sort of national goal. Such an aspiration, indeed, may never have been as deeply rooted nationally as a generation of senior politicians and bureaucrats made it appear.

On any reckoning, however, Turkey has to be considered in European terms in a way in which, say, Syria or Iraq do not. It is virtually unthinkable that it will ever be controlled by a government which is simultaneously antagonistic to the West and to Europe both politically and culturally. The most likely form of politically anti-Western government — the extremely remote possibility of a Marxist government — would almost certainly be fiercely hostile to the traditionalist and Middle Eastern elements in society, and would copy precedents created in the 1930s. Equally, when Turkish governments have contained a notable proportion of men with strongly Islamic backgrounds (e.g. in the 1950s and at present), paradoxically pro-Western policy orientations have been at their strongest.

Since the second decade of this century, Turkey's life has been dominated by problems of state-building and inculcating a unified sense of nationhood. Integration has had priority over pluralism, and nationalism over internationalism. Contacts with the West at all levels are still ambivalent. Turkish officers are required to report their contacts with all foreigners — yet their time abroad on a NATO assignment may be one of the highlights of their lives. National perspectives are expected to dominate education, and during the 1980s moves have actually been afoot to stress the national element in the teaching of history and geography in Turkish schools and to reduce the number of facts taught about the outside world. National loyalty is extolled by press and politicians. Social democrat politicians or human rights activists who complain about features of Turkish life that they find disagreeable may expect to be accused of disloyalty, if not treason. Such attitudes are of course most pronounced at a time of authoritarian rule, but they exist to some extent even under relatively liberal administrations. The *reductio ad absurdum*, encountered in some circles, is to conflate the pressures on Turkey from Western society and Soviet and other brands of communism and to see them as a combined threat to the country's independence.

These kinds of psychological and political strain upon contacts between Turkish society and the Western world are likely to persist for another generation, at least until Turkey has gone as far as Spain today in becoming an industrial and urban society. Whether or not they are ultimately exorcized depends not just on success in nation-building (which in my view is probable), but also upon deliberate policy choices by politicians, administrators and the press in Turkey and in the West. Mutual understanding will hardly be achieved while Western perceptions of Turkey ignore the dynamics of social change in the country, and while Turkey's attempts to project itself internationally continue to rely on essentially defensive stereotypes purveyed — or at least defined — by officials.

2 Political culture

Formative political experiences

History dominates political perspectives in Turkey in a way in which it does not in advanced industrial societies in the West. Furthermore, the history is not merely unfamiliar in the West; to a considerable degree it runs counter to mainstream Western views of history, since it is largely the story of encounters with Europe told from the other side.

The pre-eminent emphasis, in political speeches and newspapers as well as in school textbooks, is given to the Turkish State and the need to maintain its unity and authority. *Devlet*, the Turkish word meaning 'state', comes from the Arabic and originally meant 'dynasty'. Though there is a strain of nationalist thinking which emphasizes the 'seventeen Turkish states in history', the history of Turkey's national institutions is firmly linked to the 600-year history of the Ottoman Empire and subsequent development of the Turkish Republic. The history of the Ottoman Empire — from its apogee in the sixteenth century to its decline in the nineteenth — is usually presented in a fashion which has direct implications for the present day. The sense of being the heirs of a major world empire colours both Turkish official attitudes and, to some degree, public opinion. The question of how a state which in its heyday was more powerful than any kingdom in Christian Europe was eventually reduced to 'underdeveloped' status has preoccupied many writers on both the right and the left in Turkish politics.

During the early years of the Republic, the non-European 'oriental' and 'Islamic' features of Ottoman society were usually singled out as responsible for the decline of the Empire. The foundation of the Republic in 1923 and the Atatürk reforms were usually treated as a dramatic and deliberate historical discontinuity, albeit one which brought the Turkish people back into contact with truer 'pre-Islamic traditions'. Since 1980, the official tendency has been to stress the underlying continuity of the Empire and the Republic.

Turkey's isolationist economic policies since 1928 are a reaction against experiences of the previous century, a reaction common to both left and right. High tariff barriers, economic autarky, and a drive for heavy industry and national economic self-sufficiency – all these are the instruments which nationalist bureaucrats believed to be the only way of preventing a 'second invasion' by Western traders of the kind which, after 1882, forced the failing Ottoman Empire to place many of its public utilities under the control of a foreign debt administration.

Equally influential have been the lessons drawn from political and diplomatic history, which also emphasize defensive and isolationist responses. The disruptive effect of non-Turkish nationalisms – and the European liberalism which generally supported them – are evident to any student of late Ottoman history. The story of the break-up of the Empire is one which Turks know not merely through regular television and newspaper features; it is in many cases their own family background, the event which forced their grandparents or great-grandparents to leave their homes and settle within the borders of the Republic. The disruptive effects of separatist nationalism are usually linked to the expansionist aims of foreign powers.

The most extreme example of the possible outcome of such pressures, and the eventual reaction against it, is the story of the 1920 Treaty of Sèvres, which would have parcelled Anatolian Turkey into several non-Turkish states, and the revolt in Anatolia in 1919 against the war settlement, which led to the establishment of the Turkish Republic. The foundation of the Republic (1923) and the fifteen-year presidency of Kemal Atatürk (d. 1938) are generally presented as the fulfilment of a need to alter the forms of state government in order to ensure national independence and survival. However, along with the idea that traditionalist institutions were less rational than European ones and so a source of weakness (the basic theme behind the attack on religious and social traditionalism in the 1920s and 1930s), there also emerged the idea that Turkey had been vulnerable to threats from Europe because it lay outside Europe. If Turkey were to enter fully into the community of European nations, rather than straddle its frontier ambiguously as the dying Ottoman Empire had done, then its international relations would be those of an equal and there would be no question of threats to national independence. This second idea helps explain the major discontinuity in the foreign policy of the Turkish Republic after 1946, when Turkey dropped the twenty years of neutralism which had prevailed from 1924 onwards and opted for an explicit alliance with the West in general and the United States in particular. The switch in policy was of course more immediately provoked by Stalin's refusal to renew the Non-Aggression Pact of 1924 and by his territorial demands upon Turkey.

For the whole period before the 1973 oil shock, Turkish foreign policy was largely dominated by the need to contain the potential threat from its Russian neighbours, and also by the need to respond to a much older pattern of encroachment from the West. Defensive modernization entailed, or seemed to entail, changes throughout society. For about five decades the dominance of the 'thoroughgoing Westernizers' was clear-cut. Those who had advocated, like Mehmet Akif Ersoy in the 1920s, that Turkey should adopt the technology but not the values and culture of the West were relegated to the sidelines. None the less, there was always a certain ambivalence towards manifestations of Western life which seemed to conflict with religious or national values, such as pop culture or Christian evangelizing, especially the latter. In the 1980s, however, it was clear that inside the ruling Motherland Party there were individuals who saw Turkey's destiny in terms of cultural traditionalism combined with technological adaptation. It was not clear whether this was more than a minority view.

By contrast with the West, the Islamic world had until very recently relatively few lessons to offer. The Revolt in the Desert of 1916, and the earlier and bitterly resented need to send conscript soldiers to the Yemen, seemed simply to indicate the need for a parting of ways. To Turkish observers since the nineteenth century, the Islamic world seemed in decay and the inflexible traditionalism of the clergy was a source of danger. To the westernized bureaucratic and military middle class which emerged in the second half of the nineteenth century and whose successors still dominate the country, there was a double threat from Islamic institutions: they were directly and implacably opposed to the life-style of the new social groups, and they were also witting or unwitting allies of Western imperialism. The alliance of the Sultan and a large section of the senior clergy with the British occupiers of Istanbul after 1919 explains the uncompromising secularist policies of the 1920s and 1930s, when for a decade and a half all religious education was abolished, dervish convents suppressed, and most public cultural manifestations of Islam either outlawed or discouraged. It was, as we shall see, not until the 1960s that a serious debate on the role of Islam in Turkish society could be resumed.

Along with the emphasis on economic autarky and secularism, the Turkish Republic has consistently been concerned to promote linguistic and cultural homogeneity. This again is a reaction to the experiences of the nineteenth century and an awareness of the potential for disorder that still exists. It is hard to imagine today that a hundred years ago the population of a town like Ankara was divided approximately equally between Muslim Turks, Orthodox Greeks and Catholic or Gregorian Armenians. A country divided in this way and consequently overwhelmed by ethnic and national disputes which still seem incapable of peaceful solution may be excused for having little time for the encouragement of minority cultures and for trying to promote uniformity. The outward homogeneity of the Turkish landscape today conceals memories of upheaval and migration during the last hundred years. (The proportion of urban and middle-class Turks whose grandparents came as refugees from the Balkans, Crete, Egypt, the Caucasus or other parts of the Soviet Union is probably well over 50 per cent.) This makes for a fierce defensiveness vis-à-vis Greece or the Soviet Union. It is also the source of political complications inside Turkish communities. Many a village or small town which looks completely tranquil to the visitor is in fact split between 'locals' and 'migrants' (*yerli* and *göcmen*), who distrust each other and seldom or never intermarry.

The two potentially most serious and disruptive cleavages in Turkish society are the existence of a minority of perhaps 6–8 million Kurds, who form a majority in six south-eastern provinces which border Iraq, Iran and Syria, and of a Shi'ite or Alevi population whose numbers can only be guessed at. Before 1980, Kurdish separatist groups, mostly Marxist, had emerged in the south-eastern provinces and — although it would appear that they did not have the support of a majority of the local population — in 1977 they won control of the municipality in the principal city of the region, Diyarbakır. Since 1980, the government has returned to the policies of uncompromising efforts at assimilation. Kurdish newspapers (written in a Latin script peculiar to the Kurdish speakers of Turkey) have vanished. The new constitution and the Political Parties Law of 1983 have made it an offence to attempt to use Kurdish (though the language is not specifically named) in schools, or for broadcasting, publishing or most public meetings. The potential appeal of Kurdish nationalism is hard to estimate. It is probably very much less great than observers outside Turkey tend to suppose. Nevertheless, it has been responsible for the most serious law-and-order problems that the government has had since 1980, which culminated in the military incursion into Iraq in May 1983 and a series of clashes between guerrillas and soldiers in south-eastern Turkey between August and October of 1984, in which at least 29 Turkish soldiers were killed. For the Turkish government, the issue threatens both the unity and the security of the state itself and no compromise is possible. Sympathy for the Kurdish-speaking population, on the other hand, has been high on the list of factors bringing West European liberals and socialists into confrontation with Turkey. In late 1984, for example, Turkey formally protested at the use of the expression 'Kurdistan' by the French foreign minister.

Constitutional traditions

Representative forms of government have been associated with the drive for modernity in Turkey since the late 1870s. Since 1946, largely because of Turkey's alignment with the United States and the West, competition between political parties and free general elections have been regarded as the essential basis of the Grand National Assembly. The Assembly itself, however, has a much longer history and was important in its own right before the establishment of multiparty democracy. It was notable that in 1980 the military chose to run Turkey from the Grand National Assembly building and that, like their predecessors in 1960, they felt obliged to nominate a consultative assembly to take the place of parliament.

The way in which the National Assembly is constituted — and the degree of free popular participation involved — has been the subject of successive political experiments: in 1876, 1908, 1924, 1950, 1971 and 1982. At present the rights of political association in Turkey are very much more limited than in other European countries, and the Constitutional Court has the right to shut down political parties on a wide range of grounds, some of them simply administrative and procedural. Discussion of a range of topics — seen as critical to national unity or the survival of the state — is explicitly forbidden in the 1983 Political Parties Law. These extend, for example, to proposals to change the Turkish flag or national anthem.

Despite these curbs, it is important to understand that a member of the Turkish parliament wields considerably more patronage and influence than (for example) a Westminster MP. A Turkish deputy or senior party official will be expected to intervene in the bureaucracy much more actively and frequently than his Western counterparts, and to a certain extent individual intervention of this kind replaces some of the political functions exercised by pressure groups in most industrial democracies. On the other hand, Turkish deputies, although elected by particular provinces, do not represent them. Each one represents the entire nation.

The history of the presidency of the Republic contains fewer variations. The president acts as a mediator between the different arms of the state, explicitly so when he chairs the National Security Council, which since 1961 has acted as a forum in which military and civilian leaders meet directly. The president acts as a guardian of state traditions and institutions and does not have an executive role, although since 1982 he has wielded considerably extended powers: for example, the right to appoint candidates to many senior public positions and to dismiss cabinet ministers at the request of the prime minister. This power was in fact used in the autumn of 1984. With the exception of the special case of President Kenan Evren in 1982, who was deemed to have been elected by the referendum vote that approved the Constitution and so may arguably be eligible as a candidate in 1989, the Turkish president is not elected by popular suffrage but within the Grand National Assembly from among its own members. This appears to be intended to prevent the emergence of a president (such as Turkey in effect had between 1950 and 1960) from outside the military and civilian bureaucracy who represents a party political movement. All

Turkey's presidents other than the exception already mentioned have had a military background, and all but two have been former Chiefs of General Staff. The need to bridge the gap between this background and the requirement that a presidential candidate come from within parliament was met before 1980 by the existence of a quota of nominated senators. In the 1970s, the bicameral parliamentary system and the balloting system made it difficult to obtain either a two-thirds or a simple majority for the election of a president. To some extent the political parties, as well as the bureaucratic elite, seem to have preferred a neutral military candidate for head of state and to have been consistently unable to agree on a satisfactory civilian choice for president. The 1982 Constitution says that a written proposal of one-fifth of the Grand National Assembly will permit the nomination of a candidate from outside parliament. It can confidently be predicted that this method will be employed in 1989, thereby avoiding the deadlock which left Turkey without an elected head of state for nearly six months before the 1980 military takeover.

The military and civilian bureaucracies

As has already been suggested, the history of Turkey over the past century and a half is largely the history of the rise and expansion of its westernized middle class. Until very recently this has been in essence a 'state-service middle class' comprising military and civilian wings. Employees of the state still make up about 35 per cent of Turks with jobs in sectors other than agriculture.

In April 1908, when the western civilian intellectuals of Istanbul were threatened by an uprising of the Islamic clergy which might have restored the abolutism of Abdülhamit II, they were saved by the intervention of the army of Thessalonica. It was this experience which shaped the subsequent alliance between the military and civilian bureaucracies and determined the principle features of the reforms of the Young Turks, and after them of Kemal Atatürk. Just as they had combined against the Islamic clergy and the Palace, so the military and civilian bureaucracies would unite in emergencies to beat off challenges from other social groups to the political and social order they were trying to establish. The revolution of 1960 falls clearly into this pattern.

With the emergence of urbanized mass society in the 1960s, however, the alliance came under new strains. While the higher bureaucracy remained closely allied to the military, groups such as schoolteachers, academics and minor officials came under the influence of egalitarian and socialist ideas. During most of the 1960s, civilian bureaucrats tended to assume that the military would still be their natural allies, but the values of the military — essentially hierarchical and nationalist — asserted themselves in the military intervention of 1971. Moves towards a leftist military coup which would have brought a group of intellectuals and left-wing officers to power were brushed aside like cobwebs, and the essentially conservative nature of the military role in politics was revealed. In 1980 the military attempted for the first year of their intervention to maintain a balance between left and right (and indeed they had enemies among most of the major civilian right-wing groups), but opposition to the left became a steadily more pronounced feature of their rule as time advanced.

The cult of Kemal Atatürk as the embodiment of the Turkish Republic and its values is the hallmark of the military-bureaucratic alliance. Among its chief advantages has been the prevention of the 'Bonapartism' widely predicted by Turkish social scientists and the cult of any living personality. On the other hand, it should be noted that since the 1930s the civilian bureaucracy has been replaced as senior partner in the alliance by the military, and that many doctrines of Kemal Atatürk (most notably that of the strict separation of civilian and military offices) have fallen into obscurity. Atatürk today, in contrast to the practice during his lifetime, is often portrayed in military uniform.

Turkey no longer appears vulnerable to conspiracies by junior or middle-ranking officers. The 1960 military revolution was led by officers close to commander level. The 1971 and 1980 military interventions were organized by the Chief of General Staff of the day, and there was a striking absence of major purges of the officer corps (though some small ones were privately rumoured) after 1980. Officers in the armed forces retain their cohesion and discipline (for instance, their contacts with foreigners are restricted), and vigilance to identify the leftists, who before 1960 were common, is reputed to be intense. The education that is given to the officer corps, which usually starts in the early teens, marks them off from the rest of the population. A gruelling and harsh educational process reinforces the feeling officers have that their career is based on sacrifice for their country. During the prime of life, however, their pay-scales and living conditions are substantially better than those for their civilian bureaucratic counterparts, and the Armed Forces Mutual Assistance Fund (OYAK) gives officers security in retirement. The quality of officers' clubs has also improved in recent years, sometimes reaching the level of luxury hotels. All this has given the Turkish officer corps a strong sense of identification with the status quo. The discontent of the 1950s, when the officers were humiliated by their low salaries, is now hardly even a memory.

By contrast, the civilian bureaucracy has lost political power and economic prosperity. The conditions of the single-party period of the 1930s are distantly remembered as a golden age for bureaucracy. More recently, resentment at economic displacement and the shrinking of real incomes caused the *memur* (i.e. civil service) vote to go *en masse* to the Populist Party in a reaction against Turgut Özal during the 1983 general elections. Parts of the higher bureaucracy remain allies of the military, but many of its members are now broadly identifiable with political parties.

The expansion and contraction of popular participation

The legal and constitutional settlement of 1982 and 1983 may pose problems for Turkey in its future relations with the West. The restrictions imposed then seem stark by European standards. For example, Turks without primary education or who have been sentenced to a gaol term of a year or more, or those convicted of involvement in 'ideological and anarchistic activities', cannot be elected to parliament, 'even if they have been pardoned'. They are also, at least in theory, unable to obtain such things as driving licences. Judges, teachers and civil servants cannot stand for election unless they resign from office. Parties may not have links with trade unions and cannot advocate religious, sectarian, personal, family or interest-group policies. (Attempting to secure the domination of one social class over another has been a major criminal offence since 1931 under legislation borrowed from the Italian penal code.)

Recent Turkish history suggests a series of waves of expansion and contraction of political participation in which restrictions upon such issues as freedom of association have been alternately imposed and lifted. At regular intervals since the 1920s, Turkey's bureaucratic elite has encouraged the formation of political parties, trade unions, universities, private associations and press, and then, when these threatened to step beyond permitted limits, imposed sanctions to prevent them from doing so. Turks are accustomed to view their own political situation within a (usually over-optimistic) periodicity created by this alternation. It would seem that in the pre-1945 period, Turkey's military and bureaucratic elite created an institutional framework inside which political parties, trade unions, associations, etc., began to develop. In most cases up to 1960, they were formed as a result of prompting from above. For example, Türk-İş, Turkey's main trade-union confederation, was set up by a government initiative in 1952 — partly, no doubt, as a response to Turkey's growing involvement with the Western world and particularly the United States, but also because there were various practical purposes which made trade unions seem necessary to the government of the day. It was not till 1964 that trade unionists were given the right to strike in Turkey, and even after that date Türk-İş continued to play what is sometimes described as a 'corporatist' role, acting as the recognized representative of labour in tripartite negotiations on wages between the government, employers and workers. In recent years, Türk-İş has negotiated direct with the government, and its skirmishing with employers has been relatively unimportant. This may make the present system of trade unionism, despite all the safeguards built in by legislation, not very durable. The government is less well placed to present itself as a well-intentioned go-between between bosses and workers, and the success or failure (in recent years usually failure) of union leaders in securing advantages for their members stands out more starkly than in the past.

During the 1930s, fear of a reversion to Islamic traditionalism — symbolized in the famous clash at Menemen in Western Anatolia between a young officer and a rioting crowd led by dervishes — was the major brake upon the expansion of popular participation. Since 1970, however, the gap between the now socially much more advanced (and secularized) lower classes and the middle classes (who have greatly diversified and expanded in numbers) has narrowed. Although the 1982 Constitution prohibits theocratic, i.e. ultra-Islamic, activity, the main thrust of the restrictions it has introduced is clearly aimed at disruptive forces from another direction. Twenty years ago Dankwart Rustow noted:

> What is now at stake is not just the restructuring of a limited political elite; rather, the issue now is no less than the admission to full political participation of the lower classes in the cities and of the peasant masses in the Anatolian villages — in short, the breaking of the power monopoly held by the urban educated class since classical Ottoman days.[1]

Rustow went on to question whether Turkish 'political developments will proceed as smoothly and in as much internal peace as they have in the past'.

But this is a large and complex central theme, and it seems here worth making just two points. First, by and large, the degree of state regulation affecting parties, associations and pressure groups appears to be increasing rather than decreasing — as judged, for example, by legislation after 1980 — and those trade unions, associations and pressure groups which seemed unamenable to state regulation have not been permitted to survive. Second, this has happened because much of the new political activity which emerged in Turkey after 1960 was explicitly 'anti-system', and sought not simply to replace elitist forms of government with more broadly based ones, but was radically Marxist and anti-traditionalist in tone.

The most natural channels for enlarged political participation, the two major parties, failed to carry out this role adequately. By 1980, dramatically new patterns of social and political mobilization had emerged which were a direct threat both to the old political parties and to the constitutional system. On the right, radical nationalist groups were fighting physically with their leftist opponents for territorial control of streets, local communities and some government agencies. In the

---

[1] 'The Development of Parties in Turkey', in Joseph La Palombara and Myron Werner, eds., *Political Parties and Political Development* (Princeton, N.J.: Princeton U.P., 1966), p. 133.

industrial shanty towns, however, a variety of revolutionary Marxist underground groups seemed to have achieved an ascendancy that was based partly on their youthful political following but also on the use of violence. There were perhaps as many as fifty such groups, most of them hostile to each other, scattered across the country. It appeared likely that these had eroded the previous political dominance of the Republican People's Party (in its post-1967 social democratic clothing) in working-class areas. But the 1981 elections which would have tested this were never held.

Parliament and political parties

On 16 October 1981, thirteen months after the military revolution, Turkey's political parties were abolished. The formation of political parties was not permitted until the end of April 1983, after the passage of a new Political Parties Law, which seemed designed to make it as difficult as possible to establish parties and gave the public prosecutor sweeping powers to close down any that overstep clearly specified limits. Among the restrictions is one that forbids the re-establishment of pre-coup parties under another guise.

The attempt at a clean break was surprising, since Turkey's major parties, whatever the dates of their foundation, represent political traditions which go back to at least 1908. The abortive attempt to suppress the Democrat Party after its overthrow in the 1960 revolution seems to indicate the futility of such efforts. Although some of the DP's leadership were permanently placed on the sidelines, a recognizable successor swiftly emerged in the Justice Party.

Predictably there have been efforts to create successors to the pre-1980 parties. The Justice Party is now perpetuated in the True Path Party of Mr Hüsamettin Cindoruk, which has ably fought off an attempt to have it shut down by the Constitutional Court. Two, possibly three, successors have emerged to the centre-left Republican People's Party — notably the Social Democracy Party, which won 23 per cent of the poll in the March local elections. The smaller parties from before the coup also have their successors. The Conservative Party is a replacement for the right-wing nationalist Nationalist Action Party (NAP), and the Welfare Party represents the Islamic strand in Turkish politics. Marxist parties have not re-emerged, but only because they have not been permitted to do so.

After the shock of the 1960 revolution, it took about half a decade before the process of regrouping was completed and temporary small parties had died away. It may therefore be assumed that it will be some years before the long-term pattern of Turkish party politics reasserts itself, provided, of course, that there is not another military intervention in the meantime to upset the jigsaw.

None the less, there are many striking and unexpected changes in the post-1983 political scene. The antitheses which dominated party life since 1908 seem to have lost their importance. The Social Democracy Party (Sodep) and the True Path Party, distinct in economic and political doctrines, are *de facto* almost allies on day-to-day issues, a profound contrast with the fatal inability of their pre-coup predecessors to co-operate on essentials. The ground on which Mr Özal has chosen to fight is completely unfamiliar: privatization of state industries, increased competition, the internationalization of the economy, and an implied shift politically and perhaps also culturally (though this is controversial) towards the rest of the Islamic world. All this is quite unlike the contest for political and economic advantage among farmers, organized labour, small businessmen, civil servants, the professions, etc., which was played out in the Justice Party and Republican People's Party before 1980.

It is clear that much of the success of Mr Özal's Motherland Party (MP) derives from its having offered ordinary Turks a clear chance to make a break with policies discredited before 1980. However, the party's success may prove hard to sustain if the remaining political constraints of military rule are gradually lifted and short-term economic expectations dominate political priorities as they did for most of the period between 1950 and 1980. In that case a return to the inflationary policies practised by Adnan Menderes and later Süleyman Demirel – or possibly some kind of social democratic variant – might be expected. It is by no means certain that this will be permitted to happen.

A further question hangs over the Motherland Party itself, hastily forged by Mr Özal out of diverse political elements in the March to May period in 1983. During the party's first year in office, there was frequent press discussion of the 'four different tendencies' out of which the party had been formed, notably some right-wing nationalists from the former

NAP, and an Islamic wing from the former National Salvation Party (NSP) – including of course the premier himself. Mr Özal has proved a much more adroit party manager than most Turkish leaders. His followers in the MP in any case joined him at a time when it did not seem likely that he would win the subsequent general elections. There is thus less reason to question the strength of their adhesion to Mr Özal and his policies than is sometimes realized in Turkey. None the less, the MP has few roots. Its durability in hard times – or without Mr Özal – is very questionable. At the local level, it is uncertain whether it has succeeded in displacing the networks of patronage and clientelistic influence which looked, over three decades, to the Democrat Party and the Justice Party. So in the longer term it would seem logical for Mr Özal to try to broaden the basis of his party by absorbing as many moderate centre-rightists formerly loyal to Mr Demirel as possible. During 1984, however, the non-NSP/non-NAP elements in the MP appeared generally to be somewhat opposed to the party leadership (as, for example, during the crisis which ended in the dismissal of the finance minister, Mr Vural Arıkan). For the time being, the MP looks very vulnerable to a realignment among the right which would be centred on the True Path Party and Mr Demirel's followers. There are undoubtedly many former pro-Demirel politicians and bureaucrats waiting for such a signal. But if the MP remains the only party that looks as if it can supply political stability and economic growth, it is possible that alternative traditions on the right will gradually wither away.

On the left of centre, weak and divided leadership makes it unlikely that any single party will regain the electoral plurality held by the Republican People's Party in the 1970s. Sodep, the Social Democracy Party, seems most likely to emerge as the RPP's successor, although its failure to win control of major cities in the March 1984 municipal elections makes it vulnerable to challenges from the left. In the longer term, it may be embarrassed by a revival of left-wing underground activity, which may raise questions about Sodep's own right to exist. (Such questions were repeatedly asked about the old RPP in the early 1970s.) If Mr Özal's economic policies do eventually arouse a major popular reaction, Sodep would be the most likely beneficiary in the major cities. Whether its leaders are equipped to take advantage of this and present themselves as plausible candidates for power in the next elections is open to question.

Islam versus the secularists

In the early 1980s, educated Turks tended to pooh-pooh Western anxieties about a possible Islamic upsurge in Turkey, regarding this as an ill-informed extrapolation from events in neighbouring Iran. By the middle of the decade, they were less sure. A number of trends – notably the appearance of middle-class veiled women – seemed to be challenging the assumption that as Turkey became more industrial, urban and modern, it would also be more secular and Western in its cultural attitudes.

There was general agreement that any kind of clericalist insurrection or takeover of the kind seen in Iran was out of the question in Turkey in the 1980s. It was rather a question of whether certain elements in Turkish society were gaining a renewed Islamic coloration and changing their cultural and political orientation as a result. This suggestion was particularly disturbing to those who had assumed that Turkey's eventual goal was to be a European society, broadly compatible and comparable with that of Britain, France or West Germany. The question of religion, in whatever form it appeared, was potentially very divisive because of the intense secularist and anti-religious commitment felt by some Turks ever since the 1920s.

Several factors seem to lie behind recent changes. One is that, since 1960, the westernized elite has felt increasingly able to coexist with Islam, as shown, for instance, by the new willingness to permit clericalist parties such as the pre-coup NSP. Indeed, after the 1980 coup, sections of the bureaucratic elite felt the need actually to increase the degree of moderate traditionalist religious education in schools as an antidote to left-wing currents. Thus the 1982 Constitution goes so far as to make Islamic religious education compulsory in all schools. It must be stressed, however, that this is not the sort of full-blooded, traditionalist religious education which the Demirel government was planning to introduce in 1980, which would have involved formal Arabic instruction and a much greater degree of clerical involvement.

A second consideration is the deliberate reintroduction of vocational education for the clergy after 1965 by the Demirel governments. By 1984 about one in every ten students in secondary education was at some form of clerical school. In many ways it is surprising that the impact of this investment in religious education has been so limited.

A third influence, obviously, was developments in the Middle East. This was not confined to the revolution in Iran, which showed that groups which had seemed doomed to be historical losers could emerge as victors; it extended, from the 1960s onwards, to the considerable efforts that the major Islamic powers of the Middle East seem to have invested in trying to promote religious activity in Turkey. In terms of attendance at mosques, Turkey is still very much more religious than any West European or North Mediterranean society. Furthermore, religious and national identities remain closely intertwined. It is impossible to imagine a Turkish agnostic or atheist choosing to declare himself as such on his identity documents.

The explosive overlap of religious and political divisions was most clearly seen in Turkey in the sectarian rioting which afflicted Central Anatolian towns between 1978 and 1980, when left-wing Shi'ites of the Alevi sect came to blows with right-wing Sunnis – a reminder of the fact that between 15 and 20 per cent of the population belongs to non-Sunni, heterodox Islamic sects. Equally, the religious barrier remains the most potent force that separates Turkish public opinion from that of Europe. It is also the source of much misunderstanding of European societies.

Against this, however, it must be said that the predominant trend in Turkish urban life is clearly towards rapid secularization, especially among the young working-class. The spread of Western life-styles and habits is proceeding very fast, and the appearance of a new kind of veiled woman seems most likely to be a reaction to this (its causes are endlessly discussed by Turks). The pious background of the present prime minister, and many of his closest aides and associates, in any case suggests that while a stronger Islamic coloration might place strains on Turkey's cultural ties with Western Europe, it would not necessarily imply any sort of social or economic regression.

The present upturn in Islamic activity in Turkey is too new to permit firm conclusions about how far it will go. The underground religious brotherhoods (*tarikats*) which fuel it have no public existence, and their strength and long-term aims can only be guessed at. It is probable that, as with groups on the left, for example, their membership shifts and changes. By the mid-1980s, Turkey still looked much more likely to evolve towards greater secularism than go in any other direction, even if this evolution was turning out to be less straightforward than might have been predicted a generation earlier.

The prospects till 1989

In 1989, President Evren's seven-year term of office will come to an end. A year before that, general elections are due. It seems likely that in the meantime Mr Özal will continue in office, commanding a satisfactory majority (23 seats) in the 400-member, single-chamber Assembly. Calls for early elections by some of the opposition parties, especially those outside parliament, are likely to be ignored. The two opposition parties inside parliament are likely to become steadily weaker and more divided, and some of their members will probably align themselves with the True Path Party or Sodep as the next elections approach. As already noted, this picture of guaranteed stability would alter if (a) a strong groundswell of opposition to Mr Özal's economic policies develops or (b) the MP breaks up. All that can be said at this stage is that Mr Özal's first year in office suggested that he has a better chance of succeeding on both these fronts than some of his critics predicted.

During 1984, martial law was lifted in 33 provinces. This, rather than anything else, is evidence that Turkey is in some kind of transition towards more fully democratic conditions. The gradual relaxation of martial law can be expected to continue, which implies that it will be completely lifted in the three major cities of Ankara, Istanbul and Izmir. Just how soon this can happen is hard to say; most Turks would probably not expect such a development before 1986 or 1987. The eventual lifting of martial law in Istanbul will enable the legislation and institutions of the 1982 settlement to be fully tested for the first time. For example, martial-law press censorship would end, and the 1983 Press Law would operate. Turkish journalists find it hard to predict what this change will mean in practice. It may be the prelude to a more bumpy period in which freedoms are tested out by experiment and litigation.

It is less likely that martial law will be lifted in the provinces of south-eastern Turkey where, since August 1984, the authorities seem to have been faced with serious security problems. The nature and extent of these are largely unknown, although 29 deaths of soldiers were announced in a three-month period. If the security situation in the south-east remains serious, it will probably check whatever tendencies there are nationally towards liberalization and heighten suspicions that foreign interference (either from the Eastern bloc or from the West) could potentially lie behind the disturbances.

The press, human rights and trade union issues which have complicated Turkey's relations with Western Europe are likely to persist. They will be less inflammatory if the government chooses to move only against Marxist groups. During 1984, however, the indications were that any form of critical opposition was sufficient to invite prosecution (as shown, for example, in the trial of 56 organizers of a petition for greater liberalism that was sent to President Evren). There is no sign of a thaw on such matters at the moment, and it must be assumed that, although international press attention — and hence political repercussions — is likely to be slight, they will at least retard the growth of closer relations between Turkey and Western Europe, particularly at the parliamentary level. In short, Turkey seems set on a period of relatively dynamic economic development, coupled with a certain political isolationism. While medium- and long-term prospects remain somewhat uncertain, there is short-term stability. This is a considerable improvement on the situation in the 1970s.

Conclusion

There are striking differences between the course of Turkish and West European history, and the social and economic profile of Turkey is still markedly different even from that of such countries as Portugal. On the other hand, the history of Turkey in the twentieth century has been one of growing convergence with — and increasing involvement with — the life of Western Europe. Turkish traditions of statecraft incline its bureaucratic and military elite to be somewhat suspicious of the outside world, and this attitude is transmitted to public opinion. For various reasons, although parliamentary government seems to be strongly rooted in Turkish national life, many of the other institutions on which political pluralism depends are weak or even somewhat artificial. In the last resort, a bureaucratic and military elite remains the ultimate repository of authority in the country, and the 1982 Constitution and associated legislation are intended to make this situation permanent.

These and other, by Western standards, relatively anachronistic features of Turkish life are probably justifiable in terms of the need to maintain stability and order during a period of rapid industrialization and urbanization. It is generally assumed that another generation of industrialization will both lessen social tensions and force the development of a more flexible and well-integrated set of political institutions. That said, there remain conspicuous differences which are likely to prove awkward if, for example, Turkey attempts to move closer to the European Community. These are apparent in religious and political freedom, ethnic questions, and the clash between the essentially nationalist political philosophy embodied in Turkish institutions and the anti-authoritarian pluralist outlook which largely dominates political life in the West.

Recent trends in Turkish history are conflicting. The 'economic opening-up' to the outside world since 1980 may imply greater convergence with the West, but it has been accompanied by new political tensions. The tendency towards greater liberalism which could be observed from 1924 to 1961 in Turkey's constitutional development seems to have been replaced in 1971 and 1982 by a trend towards more authoritarian government and stricter curbs on political participation. Furthermore, these changes have taken place alongside developments (such as the gaoling of the Turkish Peace Association or the prosecution of Jehovah's Witnesses) which imply a calculated disregard for Western liberal opinion, a kind of isolationist self-assertion.

The strong role still played by religion in Turkish national life contrasts with the post-religious, or secular, atmosphere of Western countries. There is also a perceptible undercurrent of anti-Western feeling, though this is probably less strong today than it was two decades ago.

Against all this, on the Turkish side, it does seem that there is something of a national consensus about the aspiration to achieve closer links and psychological parity with the Western world in general and Europe in particular. In the long run – given that the basic aim of Turkish foreign policy is to avoid falling into the Russian orbit – close links with the West would be required even if there were not the gravitational pull of strong economic connections and powerful cultural attraction. Regrettably the climate of discussion in which the issues linking and dividing Turkey and its Western partners could be coolly examined does not yet exist. Much of the information in Western Europe about Turkey is too simplistic or even outdated to spotlight reliable long-term choices. Inside Turkey, discussions about relations with the West tend to be strident, short-sighted and emotional. Those few Turks who are well placed to inform Turkish public opinion on controversial issues in relations with the West – one thinks in particular of Mr Mehmet Ali Birand of the newspaper *Milliyet* – are usually forced to do so in polite signals and hints from the sidelines.

3 The economy

Progress towards industrialization

All attempts to map out the future of Turkey's relations with the West rely on an appraisal of its economic progress. Obviously, if in the year 2000 Turkey is approaching, say, the level of industrialization achieved a decade or two earlier by Spain, it will enjoy influence and political options which it does not have so long as its economic dealings with the West are essentially those of a borrower rather than a strong trading partner.

Despite Turkey's much publicized payments difficulties in the late 1970s, the country has shown a continuing upward trend. For ordinary Turks, impressed by improvements in their living standards over a generation or less, this eclipses Western arguments about economic mismanagement, inflationary deficit financing and chronic indebtedness. As a recent commentator observes,

> Since the foundation of the Republic Turkey's economic life has been transformed. At the beginning of the 1920s she had virtually no mechanized industry and few modern communications. All but a fraction of her people were illiterate . . . By 1980 the population had increased more than threefold and the national income almost fourteenfold over the levels of 1927.[2]

The same writer notes that national income has had a 'long-run historical growth rate since the 1930s' of 6 per cent and, given reasonably favourable external conditions, may be expected to continue at this rate

[2] William Hale, *The Political and Economic Development of Modern Turkey* (London: Croom Helm, 1981), p. 254.

or even faster till the end of the century, although debt repayment may be a short-term brake on growth. Even during the early 1980s, when the annual increases of 6–7 per cent in GNP seen during the sixties and early seventies were not achieved, growth averaged over 4 per cent, and in 1984 and 1985 it is likely to be around 4 to 5 per cent.

The past twenty-five years have seen a dramatic transformation in the structure of the economy, as the following figures show (sectors as percentage of GNP):

	1960	1965	1970	1975	1980	1983
Agriculture	37.9	31.0	26.2	22.5	22.0	17.9
Industry	15.9	19.6	22.3	24.4	24.5	27.0
Services	42.7	44.4	46.8	47.9	46.1	48.9

Population and regions

During the same period the population has grown from 27.7m to 48m, and the urban population has risen from around 25 per cent to nearly 50 per cent. The population of the largest city, Istanbul, has risen from 800,000 in 1940 to over 5m in the mid-1980s. Twenty-five cities have populations of over 100,000 compared with nine in 1960.

As in other industrializing Mediterranean countries, a severe regional disparity has developed, in Turkey's case between the western regions and those of the south-east in particular and the east in general. The backward regions have a much higher birth rate than the more developed provinces. There has been a notable slackening of the birth rate in the country as a whole in recent years from the peak of 2.8 per cent in the 1950s, and it is currently estimated at 2.1 per cent. The population is, however, likely to pass 65m by the end of this century, and the need to absorb more than 400,000 entrants to the labour market each year dominates the perspectives of planners.

Government and industry

Industrialization in Turkey, as in many late-modernizing countries, has followed an explicit governmental decision. With the emergence of a second generation of private-sector industries, however, the future of the original state industries, set up in the 1930s and afterwards, has become problematic. The role of government and of the State Economic Enterprises (SEEs) in the economy remains considerable. State involvement in industry was originally established during the 1930s and 1940s in such areas as cement, iron and steel, textiles, glass and ceramics, and the scope of its involvement has expanded even under governments notionally opposed to it. During the last eight years, the state in Turkey has gone into tyre manufacturing (despite the existence of four private-sector producers), civil and military electronics, machine tools, diesel engine production, and even aircraft manufacture. Nearly 60 per cent of banking transactions take place in the state banks (notably the Ziraat Bankası and the Türkiye İş Bankası), which are one of the major tools at the disposal of any government. In 1982 the SEEs accounted for 34.2 per cent of employment in manufacturing industry and for 25 per cent of industrial output. Investment by the SEEs was around 32 per cent of total investment (the share has risen sharply since the mid-1970s because of the decline of private-sector investment) and 55.1 per cent of public investment.

Since 1980 the government has committed itself to cutting subsidies and reducing overmanning in the SEEs. Even so, the financing requirements of the SEEs remain high: over $2,000m in 1982 and 1983. Criticism of the SEEs has produced some other changes over the past decade. Some of the newer ventures, such as Aselsan, the military electronics corporation, are run along private-sector lines and expected to make a profit. Some joint ventures have blurred the distinction between public and private sectors. The strains on the economy since 1977, however, have worked to enlarge the role of the state. Where major corporations have failed, they have been taken over by state banks. Asılçelik, the Bursa-based special steels plant which had to be bailed out by the government in 1981, has been retained as an SEE. The half-dozen banks which became insolvent after 1982 were absorbed into the state banking system. The Özal government is, however, making some attempt to roll back the frontier of state intervention: the Ziraat Bankası was forced to sell off some profitable enterprises which it had acquired as a result of the collapse of a major industrial group. More recently it has been announced that Turkish Airways – and later perhaps some other SEEs – are to be privatized, and revenue-sharing schemes have been introduced for a few public works, such as the Bosporus Bridge and the Keban Dam.

Private-sector industry

The industrial geography of the Turkish private sector shows a very heavy skew towards Istanbul. Big business is dominated by holding companies, controlled — usually rather tightly — by families, and most of the major private banks are owned by industrial groups. Most of the older holdings are strongly oriented towards the domestic market and have begun to export in earnest only since 1980. One typical example would be the Koç Group, which achieved a turnover of a billion dollars annually by 1970, but ten years later still had exports worth less than $50 million a year. Since 1980, Koç has developed its export marketing company, previously of little significance, into one of the largest in Turkey.

Despite the painful effects of the 1980 Stabilization Programme and its aftermath (in particular high interest rates — at the time of writing a 'subsidized' export credit costs about 60 per cent, and commercial credits can be around 100 per cent net), private-sector manufacturing has continued to grow steadily during the 1980s. Basic metal industries and related metal products have been growing by nearly 20 per cent annually, and textiles and related industries by about 12 per cent. Food and beverages have grown by 7 or 8 per cent annually. Only one sector, non-metallic products, appears to have declined. In the longer term, then, the industrial profile of Turkey is becoming much more complex: food and textiles are less important; chemicals, metal industries and, latterly, electronics are gaining.

The changes introduced in 1980 will take many years to work their way through. Emphasis on research and development, for example, is relatively slight in most of the major holding groups. Although aggressive marketing and sales departments have been created inside most of the groups, trained managerial talent is insufficient to meet demand. Even so, quality control is improving, partly because the government has liberalized imports both of raw materials and specialized inputs, and of some competing end-products. The general picture, therefore, is one of surprising resilience. The motor industry (more than 20 fledgling subsidiaries of major international parent corporations) has not folded, as many predicted during the late 1970s, and rationalization is likely to be achieved gradually, with the weaker producers quietly disappearing. Passenger-car sales and output both rose during 1983 and 1984.

In other words, growth – and probably very rapid growth, by OECD standards – is likely for Turkish private-sector manufacturing if the investment climate brightens with the return of relative price stability. Although Turkey's bid to attract foreign investment has not so far yielded great results, the flow of foreign capital into the country is expected by major Western embassies to become increasingly significant in the second half of this decade.

These changes are likely to bring Turkey into the mainstream of the international business world and to place Istanbul on the map as a commercial centre to an extent unheard-of since before World War I. The political and cultural effects of this are likely to be profound. The Özal government appears to have a 'Japanese model' behind its thinking, in which a strong economy geared towards exports retains distinctive and indeed rather isolationist cultural and traditional values; but Turkey's proximity to Western Europe, and the strong inroads made by Western culture and life-style in the last hundred years, may produce different results, pulling it more firmly into the Western cultural orbit.

The internationalization of the economy

Turkey's change of economic policy from 1980 onwards appears to be a major break with previous practice. Yet during the 1960s and 1970s, the emergence of the new large-scale private industrialists of Istanbul led to calls by some sections of business for greater emphasis on foreign trading. The increased interest during the early 1970s in the question of Turkish full membership of the EC was a reflection of this. The payments crisis of the later seventies forced Turkish businessmen to realize that the import substitution policies followed since the 1930s were a blind alley. Exports and access to a large market were needed to make larger-scale production economic, as well as to provide the foreign currency earnings to finance imports of raw materials, machinery and technology. Before 1980 Turkey's earnings from agricultural exports in effect subsidized developments in manufacturing industry.

Özal's economic philosophy was shaped by his experience in the Turkish bureaucracy and in the private sector during the mid-1970s. His reforms came in two principal stages: the original stabilization package of 24 January 1980 and the changes introduced in December 1983 after his return to office as prime minister. The stabilization package had as its chief features:

(a) *Realistic exchange-rate policies.* The Turkish lira has been regularly adjusted against the dollar, and since May 1981 the rate has been announced on a daily basis.

(b) *Realistic interest rates*: these have operated since July 1980 and from 1982 onwards have generally given depositors a net return over inflation. Equally, the previously artificially low rates to borrowers have been sharply raised.

(c) *Tight control over the money supply and credit*, within the context of agreements with the IMF.

(d) *The ending of most state-sector price subsidies* and of price control boards.

(e) *A tax reform*: one was legislated in 1981 but has not proved very successful. It has been supplemented since January 1985 by a value-added tax.

(f) *The encouragement of foreign investment* and the introduction of new legislation and the creation of a unified body to handle foreign investment.

In 1983 Ozal introduced further changes:

(a) *The foreign currency regime was liberalized* and there was considerable progress towards convertibility of the lira. Turks were allowed to buy and hold foreign currency, and in late 1984 the government announced that it would accept payment for some exports in Turkish lira.

(b) *Export incentives* were made more selective and subsidies were reduced.

(c) *A partial liberalization of imports* both of raw materials and of some consumer goods, including foods.

(d) *Administrative reorganization* of the State Economic Enterprises.

(e) *A new Five-Year Plan was announced* for 1985–9.

Özal's reforms have brought impressive results. The volume of foreign trade has risen sharply. Exports have risen from $2.9bn in 1980 to $7.1bn in 1985, while imports grew less swiftly from $7.9bn in 1980 to $10.6bn in 1985. Shortages and power cuts have virtually disappeared. Capacity utilization, which was 51.2 per cent in Turkish industry in 1980, rose by 1984 to over 70 per cent. Inflation fell from three-digit levels in 1980 to 24 per cent in 1982, though it was 39 per cent in 1983, and apparently 53 per cent in 1984. Most strikingly, GNP growth was swiftly resumed: from declines of 0.4 per cent in 1979 and 1.1 per cent in 1980, GNP rose by 4.1 per cent in 1981, 4.6 per cent in 1982, 3.2 per cent in 1983 (when Özal was out of office) and an estimated 5.7 per cent in 1984.

For diplomats, international agencies and potential foreign investors the question now is whether the Özal reforms will stick or whether there will be a reversion to fixed exchange rates, protectionism and import substitution. It seems fairly clear that Mr Özal and his team will adhere to free-market and export-oriented policies as long as they remain in office. It is also apparent that the main political parties to challenge Mr Özal in the 1989 general elections will be directly opposed to much or all of the Özal platform. The Social Democrats will offer their traditional prescription of statism and protectionism. The True Path Party leadership, despite the fact that Mr Özal's programme was in-augurated under a Demirel government, is likely to urge the kind of policies seen in Turkey in the 1970s, with public spending on big indus-trial and infrastructure projects (and little concern about high inflation and monetary discipline). Both Sodep and the TPP have a sporting chance of an election victory.

In the short term, Mr Özal's perspectives are probably dominated by the social effects of his economic policies. The alleged increase in un-employment and income inequality are so far hard to measure. Contrary to general claims of impoverishment, the burden has probably been distributed unevenly, with at least some groups making gains in their real income. In 1983, according to the OECD, real incomes seem to have risen. It is unlikely that for many people they fell in 1984. Opposi-tion appears to be strongest among fixed-income groups, particularly civil servants. Fears that the austerity programme might lead to outbreaks of violence have not been borne out by events, and the law-and-order machinery set up after 1980 in any case makes disorder unlikely.

From sections of industry, on the other hand, comes a steady pressure to change course. Smaller Anatolian industrialists and traders have been understandably opposed to Özal's policies, and the Union of Chambers of Commerce and Industry, normally close to a right-of-centre government, has emerged as a source of criticism under its chairman, Mr Mehmet Yazar. Though larger-scale industrialists in Istanbul support the government, they do so with an enthusiasm which is proportionate to their role as exporters. Schemes for slowing down the depreciation of the lira or moving towards some sort of semi-fixed parity are advocated by several of the larger and older industrial groups, who still rely largely on the domestic market. So far Mr Özal has been able to ignore these. In private, however, many industrialists report that operating conditions are still very tough, and it will take several more years before the success of the Özal experiment can be regarded as guaranteed.

Debts and payments in the 1980s

Payments problems are likely to remain moderately severe, with 1984 and 1986 being 'hump years' in Turkey's debt-repayment schedule. The country will remain a borrower, probably to the tune of more than $1,000m a year, and total debts are likely to rise from $19.4bn at the end of 1984 to around $25.5bn in 1989. Although the trade balance will remain in deficit, it is likely to become steadily more manageable, and anxiety will centre on the current account, which, in the early 1980s, Özal planned to bring into equilibrium by 1984. In fact there was a current account deficit of $1.8bn that year, not a very great improvement on the $2.1bn of 1983. Worries about Turkey's medium-term current account performance prompted the International Monetary Fund during the autumn of 1984 to draw up two alternative scenarios for the Fifth Five-Year Plan, whose present growth targets (rising to over 7 per cent annually by 1988/9) are feared to mean a doubling of the current account deficit and a debt-service ratio of 22 per cent. An alternative scenario put forward by the Fund would allow the current account to balance, bring down the debt-service ratio to below 20 per cent but imply GNP annual growth of 5 per cent or less. A senior Turkish official describes this option as 'out of the question for us'. Mr Özal has for several years argued that growth will have to go up to about the 7 per cent level if it is to have any impact on Turkey's social ills, notably unemployment.

On present form, Turkey should find it possible to borrow on the scale required from commercial banks and other lending institutions. Political factors aside, debt-servicing has become almost the main policy priority of Turkish economic management, and the difference of outlook with the IMF mentioned in the previous paragraph should not obscure the fact that Turkey under Mr Özal has emerged as a model pupil in the Fund's disciplines. The willingness of ever more foreign banks, and particularly American ones, to enter a finite market, even though they are aware that this will mean participating in syndications, is encouraging. Five more years of well-managed export-oriented policies would bring the Özal experiment to the end of its first decade, and would probably have irreversible effects on the structure of manu-facturing industry and public policy.

On the other hand, any Turkish government that relies primarily on the support of voters will be under pressure to return to inflationary policies. Even at the end of the decade, per capita GNP is unlikely to be much above $1,300 at 1983 prices, and income inequality and unem-ployment are expected to have worsened. The implication seems to be that Turkey may have to choose between continuing with the economic discipline introduced by Mr Özal and progressing towards a more liberal political order. No one, however, would have predicted in 1982 that Mr Özal, then leaving office with the opprobrium following a financial crash, would be elected prime minister less than eighteen months later with, undeniably, the majority of the country behind him.

Turkey's prospects as a trading nation

During the 1960s and 1970s, Turkey was an undertrading nation. It is likely that from the end of this decade onwards it will have achieved the volume of trade characteristic of a country of its size and level of development. That will mean that the international economic environ-ment will also have an increasing effect on its economic future in a way which was not true in the past. In 1973, for example, the first oil price hike barely affected Turkey, and the country enjoyed a couple of reasonably vigorous years of growth before it ran into troubles which had more to do with domestic mismanagement than the international recession. The pattern of Turkey's foreign trade over the five years to

Pattern of Turkish trade, 1979–83 (%)

	1979	1980	1981	1982	1983
(a) EXPORTS					
OECD area	63.9	57.7	48.1	44.5	48.2
EC	48.5	42.7	32.0	30.6	35.1
West Germany	21.9	20.8	13.7	12.3	14.6
Italy	9.4	7.5	5.2	5.7	7.4
UK	4.6	3.6	3.1	3.3	4.3
France	6.1	5.6	4.6	3.4	3.2
USA	4.6	4.4	5.7	4.4	4.1
Islamic countries	n.a.	n.a.	41.6	47.8	45.8
Iran	0.5	2.9	5.0	13.8	19.0
Iraq	5.0	4.6	11.9	10.6	5.6
Libya	1.9	2.1	9.4	4.1	3.2
USSR	5.6	5.8	4.1	2.2	1.6
(b) IMPORTS					
OECD area	60.6	45.3	47.9	50.2	48.5
EC	40.7	27.8	28.2	27.9	28.1
West Germany	17.6	10.5	10.5	11.4	11.4
Italy	6.3	3.7	4.2	4.7	5.5
UK	4.4	4.0	4.9	4.9	4.8
France	7.7	4.7	4.5	1.8	2.4
USA	7.4	5.6	6.6	9.2	7.5
Islamic countries	n.a.	n.a.	40.0	42.4	39.5
Iran	3.6	10.1	5.8	8.5	13.7
Iraq	11.4	15.6	17.5	16.0	9.8
Libya	4.1	9.8	8.8	10.1	8.6
USSR	2.1	2.2	1.8	1.2	2.6

Source: Türkiye İş Bankası, 'Economic Indicators'.

1983 is set out in the table below. It will be noticed that while there has been a striking upturn in the volume of exports going to other Middle Eastern countries, the pattern is both recent and not very stable, with some strong fluctuations between trade performance in different years. Over the past decade the trend away from trade with the OECD area has been very marked: ten years ago it accounted for nearly three-quarters of Turkish foreign trade. A general diversification, however, rather than a simple shift to the Islamic world seems to be the explanation for this. Several of Turkey's principal trading partners in the Islamic world are radical regimes whose future is not easy to predict. Trade with Iran, for example, fell well below anticipated levels in 1984. So far, Turkish trade with the 'moderate states' of the Middle East is relatively modest, although in 1984 Saudi Arabia purchased 6.4 per cent of Turkish exports.

Turkey's industries, with a few exceptions — notably textiles — still operate on too small a scale to make them competitive in European markets. However, it is conceivable that in another generation a few large investments could turn parts of the motor or electronics industries into viable large-scale exporters on the Spanish model. But that depends on Turkey's success in restructuring its industries, attracting large-scale investment and transforming itself into a merchant state. Immediate objectives are much more limited, and concentrate on ensuring that the current account is kept under control and that price stability gradually returns. Under these circumstances it is hard to imagine Turkey seriously attempting to enter a customs union with the European Community in the near future, and any application for membership would be political rather than economic in motivation.

4 Foreign policy

The nature of foreign policy-making

Any consideration of ways in which Turkey might become more closely involved with the rest of its Western allies requires an assessment of the degree to which its perceived foreign policy interests overlap with those of the West in general. Even among the advanced industrial democracies of Western Europe, an assertive nationalism can make a common foreign policy difficult, as the example of France shows. In general, late-modernizing Mediterranean states seem to have different preoccupations and goals and make difficult partners. Turkey's ambiguous geographical and cultural situation means it has interests to defend — for example in the Balkans and the Middle East — and is involved in blocs — such as the Organization of the Islamic Conference — which have no direct parallels in the rest of the Western world. Do these preclude a closer relationship with the West? Do they, as is sometimes claimed, create an underlying sense of national interest in which there is a certain political agnosticism?

Although successive political parties have coloured Turkey's foreign policy to some extent, causing emphasis to shift from time to time, foreign affairs have always been treated as national rather than party-political matters. It is notable that, in the 1940s, the then president, İsmet İnönü, before deciding to go ahead with the introduction of multiparty democracy, was careful to receive assurances from the incipient civilian opposition that the basic continuity of Turkish foreign policy would not be challenged. Since 1983, foreign policy has appeared to be one of the areas of government in which President Evren retains most direct influence. In general, it seems likely that on all major questions, especially those involving strategic interests, the role of forces

41

outside the civilian government and outside the Foreign Ministry is paramount. In November 1983, for example, it is fairly clear that officials in the relevant department of the Foreign Ministry were by no means the first to learn about the impending declaration of unilateral independence by the Turkish Cypriots.

As in other late-modernizing countries, the role of public opinion in foreign policy is obtrusive, with press coverage of many topics being noisy and emotional and acting as a major constraint on the government. This is particularly the case where such issues as the Cyprus problem, disputes with Greece and relations with Europe are concerned. For the press, national prestige often appears to be a goal in itself, with headlines focusing on foreign television programmes, or irredentist maps, or hostile remarks about Turkey (though since 1981 the press has been forbidden to reprint unfavourable foreign press reports).

Despite this, the general tone of public opinion is basically pragmatic, with the possible exception (an understandable one) of attitudes towards Armenian terrorism. A certain anti-Americanism is occasionally to be found in Turkish public opinion, but it has none of the atavistic force encountered in some of Turkey's neighbours, and, even allowing for censorship, it is much weaker today than it was two decades ago.

Specialist commentators in the press — for example Fahir Armaoğlu, Mehmet Ali Birand, Hâluk Ülman — engage in discussion and debate which seems to be based on broad like-mindedness on national interests (despite their different positions over internal issues). In general the degree of understanding of Western societies, and the ability to sympathize with their perspectives and problems, are limited, and an aggrieved demand for psychological parity is often the keynote, especially during periods of strained relations with Western Europe or the United States.

Despite its visibility, the role of public opinion is in some ways narrower than in Western societies. Except among Marxists, the right of the military to act as the ultimate arbiters of national interest is unquestioned. It is unlikely, for example, that a settlement with Greece or in Cyprus would face serious challenge if it was known to have the approval of the military leadership.

Caution, based on awareness of limited resources, dominates Turkish foreign policy. The striking success in cultivating friendly relations with much of the Middle East since 1974 has been based not on grand, Kissinger-like gestures of statesmanship but on the persistent building-up of friendly diplomatic ties and the development of economic contacts. Turkey has conspicuously eschewed an active role as mediator in the Iran/Iraq war, probably because of an awareness of the fragility of its position. It has also found it easier to deal with the maverick 'rejectionist states' of the Middle East such as Libya than to make very much progress with more solidly based administrations such as that of Egypt, at least until the visit in May 1985 of President Mubarak.

The bureaucratic and nationalist background of Turkish foreign policy-makers can be a disadvantage when dealing with public opinion and other manifestations of the pluralist life of the West. A senior Turkish foreign office official once privately remarked to the present writer that he and his colleagues found it much easier to deal with countries such as Iraq or Yugoslavia, 'where the government runs things', than with public opinion in the West. Present circumstances probably accentuate this disadvantage.

Basic goals of Turkish foreign policy

Turkey's foreign policy has as its overriding objective the maintenance of the state and its independence. President Evren has said in his speeches, on several occasions, when discussing strains with Western Europe, that the 'Turkish state will continue to exist, no matter what'. A sense of encirclement by unfriendly neighbours, and of proximity to an unstable and violent area, is always evident. There was an undercurrent of shock in Turkish public opinion at the executions that began in Iran in 1979, which probably reflects a special awareness that these things were happening in an immediately neighbouring country.

As noted several times already, the fundamental problem of Turkish foreign policy since the time of Peter the Great has been that of containing Russian expansionism. Conscripts in the army are sometimes surprised at being taught that Russia — rather than any other country — is Turkey's main enemy. The surprise is probably less great among the substantial portion of the population whose families came from either present-day Soviet or Balkan territory. However, the disparity in size between Turkey and its northern neighbour means that responses to the

Soviet threat are diplomatic as well as military. 'Good neighbourliness' and the avoidance of provocation are constantly emphasized. There have been no spy scandals in Ankara comparable with those which periodically occur in Western capitals, despite the large size of the Soviet mission there. Turkey has been one of the major recipients of Soviet economic aid, and depends on imports of Soviet and Bulgarian electricity for about 7 per cent of its annual consumption. The 1.4m tonne capacity iron-and-steel plant (Turkey's third), which was opened at İskenderun in 1975, was built by the Soviets. Istanbul in a few years will be receiving natural gas from the Soviet Union, via a spur through Thrace and Bulgaria of the pipeline to Western Europe. More fundamentally, it is probable that if the Russians had not made a series of foreign policy blunders in the Middle East between 1942 and 1954, Turkey would have continued its non-aggression pact with them, and its military alliance with the West would not have acquired the momentum which it did.

The willingness of Turkey to enter a military conflict between the West and the Warsaw Pact powers is sometimes questioned. After all, the country had binding treaty commitments to Britain and France in 1939 but did not enter World War II until February 1945. Turkish officers and government officials, however, are unambiguous in stating that the country is fully committed to its obligations under NATO. These obligations, though, are perceived as reciprocal, a point which Turkey has stressed in its successive Defence and Economic Cooperation Agreements with the United States. Turkish officials tend also to be rather clear that NATO is a defensive rather than an offensive alliance, one intended to forestall conflict through vigilance.

Industrialization, originally seen as a defensive adaptation but now viewed as the completion of an already well-advanced social transformation, is another preoccupation of Turkish foreign policy-makers. The maximization of economic assistance and the removal of obstacles to trade, such as EC quota restrictions on Turkish textile exports, are typical themes. On the other hand, Turkey has not developed specialized commercial and economic services for exporters within its diplomatic services, although the importance of 'economic diplomacy', as well as that of the job of deputy under-secretary for economic affairs in the Foreign Ministry, has increased markedly since 1980.

Turkish goals in relations with the West thus seem to consist of (1) maintaining the alliance and the flow of aid which derives from it; (2) fostering opportunities for trade; (3) asserting a limited but symbolic presence in major Western political forums, and generally asserting a presence at the 'macro' rather than the 'micro' level; (4) coping with specific frictions such as the problems of migrant workers in West Germany; and (5) handling the rivalry with Greece inside NATO, the EC and other bodies. These goals are not very ambitious or dynamic ones. It is possible, for example, to imagine a Turkish administration making convergence with Europe and a stronger European awareness of Turkey a major goal, but this sort of disposition, which was most pronounced in the 1950s, appears if anything to have diminished.

Much of the governmental sensitivity towards Western Europe at the moment, sometimes played up by US diplomats, tends to be along the lines that Europe should 'drop its criticisms' on such matters as human rights. This seems more like an effort to restore diplomatic equilibrium than the prelude to increasing involvement, which may be a point on which Turkey's governmental elite is internally divided. From the outset of such controversies as the Peace Association Trials, which have done most to isolate Turkey from European opinion, it has been much easier to find officials (even military officials) who are critical of such actions than those who can make a coherent defence of them. Indeed the idea is sometimes advanced inside Turkey that trials of this sort may even be intended to be deliberate gestures of self-isolation.

The fact that Western Europe accounts for more than 40 per cent of Turkish external trade, as well as being the principal supplier of machinery and spare parts for the economy, means that economic disentanglement is virtually unthinkable. The cultural prestige of Western Europe, and the institutional links with it through bodies such as the Council of Europe and the EC, also make permanent political detachment hard to imagine. But it is possible to conceive of an economically strong and culturally isolationist Turkey allowing many of its political links with Western Europe to atrophy and relying on national solidarity to ensure that expatriate Turkish communities in Western Europe do not generate political frictions. Such a development would probably not have very much effect on Turkey's reliability as a military ally in the long run.

Foreign policy

The 1960s and 1970s were periods when Turkey felt psychologically quite 'open' to Western Europe, no doubt largely because of mass movements of its workers abroad. Since 1979, and especially with the introduction in 1980 of visa requirements for Turks travelling to most European states, there has been a sense of being blocked off from Western Europe which is intense but not easy to explain. Numbers of Turks travelling abroad have in fact risen steadily: from 802,000 in 1972 to 1.8 million ten years later. At any rate the transfusion of attitudes, mutual understanding and firsthand knowledge, on which political convergence depends, seems somehow to have been constricted.

Attitudes towards Islamic countries

The oil price hike of 1973 and the perceived isolation after the 1974 Cyprus crisis were the main factors behind Turkey's renewed interest in its Middle Eastern neighbours after half a century of indifference. In 1983 Turkey sent nearly a quarter of its exports (24 per cent) to Iran and Iraq (the former a country with which trade links had been insignificant five years earlier), and in 1984 around 40 per cent of Turkish exports went to Islamic countries (this compares with 53 per cent to the OECD group of nations).

Although it is a secular state, Turkey's Muslim national identity has permitted it to take part in the activities of the Organization of the Islamic Conference, and it has played a fairly important part in the Conference in recent years, acting as host country to its Economic Sub-Committee in November 1984. In contrast to this, despite fairly intense lobbying from Arab countries, Turkey retains vestigial diplomatic ties with Israel. However, its foreign policy line is now clearly pro-Palestinian, and since 1979 there has been a PLO mission in Ankara with diplomatic status.

In dealing with other Muslim countries, very different historical and cultural influences are called into play. In general Turkey seems to enjoy easiest relations with distant, non-Arab Muslim states such as Malaysia, with which the relationship is simply diplomatic. It has a tradition of good working relations with some Arab Middle Eastern states, notably Iraq and (not quite as smoothly) Libya, and the pragmatism of Turkish foreign policy made it fairly easy to develop effective economic relations with the Islamic revolutionary regime in Iran after 1979, even though it replaced a long-standing ally with whom Turkey had rather more in common.

There are probably strict limits to the extent to which rapprochement with the Middle East can go. For a start, the Turkish middle class is unlikely to be willing to make compromises at a cultural level, however many cosmetic gestures may be made at political meetings. The government continues to be vigilant against Islamic missionary activity by states as different as Iran, Saudi Arabia and Libya. A spate of espionage arrests, early in 1985, of prominent figures accused of spying for Libya, a close trade partner of Turkey, illustrated other dangers which had not previously been anticipated.

The paradox that Turkey gets on better with the radical Islamic states than it does with the moderates points up another lesson. If a political, and perhaps military, alliance between, say, Turkey, Egypt, Jordan and Saudi Arabia ever emerges, it will probably be the work of many years, but such an alliance is unlikely while the main theme of Turkish foreign policy is to be friends with anybody, but especially with oil-rich countries which demand its goods and services. The care Turkey has taken to maintain working relations with Iran, despite its substantial community of . interests with Iraq, is significant in this respect.

Increased military and economic strength is likely to make Turkey much more important as an actor in Middle Eastern politics; indeed, its 're-emergence' in Middle Eastern affairs is largely the result of its relative success at industrialization. Caution, however, is likely to remain the keynote. Turkey is too far distant to be able to play a major role in the defence of the Gulf, even if in some respects it appears to be a candidate for this, and its burgeoning trade links with Gulf states have made it aware of their fragility.

From the Islamic (and particularly the Arab) point of view, Turkey has two handicaps which may eventually be expected to reassert themselves. First, it is a former imperial power in the region, and although in some cases (e.g. Libya's) this is not unwelcome, it creates tensions in the arc of countries between Syria and Egypt. Second, Turkey is viewed as being highly westernized and a close ally of the United States.

Conflicts with Greece

From the point of view of the West, the rivalry between Turkey and its neighbour and ally Greece has been the most serious and intractable problem that the alliance has had to contend with in the Eastern Mediterranean. The 1974 Cyprus crisis was a major turning-point in Turkey's international relations, and triggered a Turkish search for alternative foreign policy relations to those of the preceding twenty-five years. The degree to which Turkey and Greece have conflicting interests is less striking than the historical antagonism which has created various arenas for a diplomatic and political contest between them: notably the Aegean and Cyprus. As already noted, the Soviet Union rather than Greece is traditionally considered the main external threat to Turkey (though since 1974 not necessarily the most immediate one). For two generations after the 1923 Treaty of Lausanne, which was intended to define a permanent settlement between Greece and Turkey, good relations with Athens and the avoidance of conflict were considered the most important element in Turkish foreign policy. Turkey thus acquiesced after World War II in the 1946 Treaty of Paris, which allowed the (overwhelmingly Greek-inhabited) Dodecanese islands along the Anatolian coast to be transferred from Italian sovereignty to Greek.

The attitude of successive Turkish administrations towards the various disputes with Greece is best described as legalistic, with an emphasis on reaching written treaty agreements through negotiation, while insisting that the provisions of the treaties affecting the two countries (Lausanne, Paris) be strictly adhered to. Continuing Turkish insistence on the demilitarization of the Dodecanese, usually regarded in Greece as an attempt to wrest a concession that parts of that country are not fully sovereign, represents attempts to invoke the stability of a contractual bargain. Irredentist currents in politics are not encouraged. Although the presence of the Turkish minority in Western Thrace is regarded as a foreign policy lever, the Foreign Ministry seems generally concerned to get the Turkish press to play down the issue and characteristically tries to cool overheated nationalist passions.

Public opinion in Turkey, as in Greece, has politicized such topics as the Flight Information Region in the Aegean and turned them into fiercely contested issues. Although there are some material interests at stake — access to the ports of Izmir and Istanbul through the internal waterways of the Aegean, mineral rights in the sea-bed — the contest appears to be largely over symbolic issues.

In Cyprus, on the other hand, Turkey faced after 1954, first, the risk of a major shift in the strategic balance between itself and Greece and, second, a recurrence of the type of ethnic conflict which had been settled elsewhere by the terms of the Treaty of Lausanne. Had there been no substantial Turkish minority on the island and had Greece been willing to agree to its demilitarization, 'Enosis' might have been conceivable. Neither condition in fact obtained, and a historical accident in 1974 created circumstances in which Turkey was able to impose a *de facto* solution that was intended to resolve local conflicts in line with the precedents of 1924, and to safeguard the country's strategic interests by maintaining the independence of the island.

In the subsequent search for a negotiated settlement, both Turkey and Greece have attempted to use their reluctant NATO allies to pressure the other. Turkey's superior strategic importance has been matched by the strength of the Greek community in the United States, which succeeded between 1975 and 1978 in bringing about an embargo on US military aid and sales to Turkey, the real aim of which was probably to weaken the relationship between Turkey and the West rather than simply to apply pressure for concessions in Cyprus.

The fundamental lesson of the 1974 crisis in Cyprus and its aftermath is that the strategic balance in the Eastern Mediterranean — for many years apparently fairly even between Greece and Turkey — is shifting irrevocably in the latter's favour. In 1923 there was a population difference of two or three million between the two states, and Greece — poor by European standards — was socially and economically far more advanced than Turkey. In the late 1980s, Turkey has nearly five times the population of Greece and a gross national product approximately twice as large. Its fear, strong in the early 1970s, of a pre-emptive strike by Greece is thus receding.

The Cyprus crisis of 1974 forced Turkey to make a choice between its perceived national interests and its relations with the USA and the West. In the mid-1970s came attempts to set up new military industries (for example Aselsan, the military electronics corporation) and to devise a more broadly based foreign policy. None the less, the prime emphasis on good relations with the West quickly reasserted itself and, by March 1980, relations with the USA had once more been stabilized under a new Defence and Economic Cooperation Agreement. It is hard, given the consistently cautious interpretation of national interest which has prevailed in Turkish foreign policy since 1924, to imagine any Turkish administration risking the country's overall relationship with the West in pursuit of an irredentist objective. If, on the other hand, Turkey appeared to be under even limited attack (e.g. in the Aegean) it might well move to eliminate the problem at source.

The fact that the various Western organizations of which both Greece and Turkey are members have become arenas for the contest between them is often regarded with exasperation in the West. NATO has, however, undoubtedly helped cushion the dispute between the two states since 1974, and in 1980 it played a major part in reopening the Aegean to civilian flights. During the 1950s and earlier, the existence of an international order, backed by one or more of the great powers, helped make effective working relations between Greece and Turkey easier. It is thus at least a theoretical possibility that if public opinion in both countries could be tamed, the way to a lasting resolution of antagonism between them might be a more thorough integration of both into the Western world. Put another way, Greece's apparent aim — at least as seen in Ankara — of trying to exclude Turkey from the Western world would, if it succeeded, accentuate the confrontation between the two countries while reducing the number of instruments available for diplomacy.

Armenian terrorism

Finally, in looking at Turkey's relations with the outside world, a few words need to be said about another legacy from the past: the international implications of the terrorist campaign since 1974 by a number of Armenian underground organizations against Turkish diplomats and their families abroad. The campaign — in which, to date, 41 Turks and a number of non-Turks have been murdered — has powerfully reinforced isolationist trends in Turkish opinion and has highlighted the difference between Turkish historical and political attitudes and those of some Western countries. A legitimate sense of indignation among Turks that the murder of diplomats was used by the Western media as a peg to revive stories of alleged massacre (a reference to events of 60 or 70 years earlier), sometimes in a fashion which suggested that such massacres might still be continuing, has shifted to a debate about the allegations themselves. The collision between the Turkish point of view, periodically reinforced by outrage at new assassinations, and elements of Western public opinion has been important. It has dragged down Turkish-French relations to an unprecedentedly unfriendly level and, during the autumn of 1984, it threatened to damage Turkish relations with the United States, when Congress seemed likely to approve a resolution which by implication accused Turkey of genocide. The disputes of the late Ottoman Empire spill disturbingly into the present, and accentuate the sense many Turks have of a cleavage between their country and the West. It is unlikely that these tensions – which are rooted in the self-images of several peoples – will die away for several generations at the earliest.

5 Turkey and NATO

Turkey's membership of the North Atlantic Treaty Organization is generally regarded as the key to the rest of its international relations. It joined the alliance, along with Greece, in February 1952 after two years of lobbying for admittance, and an earlier rebuff. Application for membership was a response to the communist seizure of Eastern Europe after World War II and to several years of demands on the part of the Soviet Union for the cession of three Turkish provinces and the right to station troops on the Bosporus.

From the point of view of the alliance, Turkey offered the distinct attractions of a very large land army (then eighteen divisions), at a time when perspectives were dominated by the recent Korean war, and control of the Bosporus and Dardanelles and thus of access to the Eastern Mediterranean. There was, however, some initial unwillingness among NATO members to see the alliance move from the Atlantic to the Caucasus, for logistical reasons. Moreover, Turkish entry involved some modification in the wording of the original North Atlantic Treaty, which specifically mentioned Europe. In the early 1950s at least, Turkey appeared geographically to be an Asian country. But these difficulties were eventually overcome, and Turkish membership soon stimulated important responses from the alliance: the setting up of the Command Land Forces South East (Comland SE) subcommand in Izmir and the Command Mediterranean North East (Commednoreast) subcommand in Ankara, both of which report direct to Naples.

Turkey's special regional interests, however, notably those in Cyprus, affected its notions of military integration and operational authority. As in other NATO countries, divisions allocated to NATO remain under the direct command of Turkish military authorities, except presumably in time of a war involving the alliance as a whole. But after the 1974

Cyprus crisis, Turkey, which had previously had three armies, set up a fourth, the Aegean Army, outside the NATO command structure and evidently intended to guard against possible aggression from Greece.

During the early years of Turkish membership of the alliance, there was also some unease at possible discrepancies between the 'all-out strategy to be employed by NATO' and Turkey's strategic requirements. The strategy of 'flexible response' caused particular disquiet among segments of Turkish public opinion, since it could be taken to imply that large areas of the east of the country might be sacrificed without a fight in time of war. Such disquiet appears to have faded today, possibly because a Soviet invasion through the Caucasus, despite publicity about troop movements on the other side of the border, is harder to imagine nowadays than it was in the 1950s.

This is partly because the nuclear shield, which protects Turkey along with other Western nations, makes such conventional military intervention hard to envisage. Jupiter missiles (IRBMs) were stationed on Turkish soil after Turkey joined the NATO command and remained their until the Cuban missile crisis in the early 1960s. Tactical nuclear weapons were requested by Turkey in December 1956 and were later delivered by the United States. Though under American custody, it was stressed that in time of war they would be fired by Turkish soldiers, an emphasis which continues today and enables Turkish public opinion to regard nuclear weapons on Turkish soil as being in some sense 'Turkish'.

Anxieties about the Soviet Union seem to have played a part in the evolution of Turkey's nuclear role since the Cuban missile crisis. Although nuclear weapons are believed to be stationed on Turkish territory, this fact is not usually admitted by Western officials (but curiously it sometimes is in the Turkish press). In 1965 Turkey declined to back plans to establish mixed-nationality Polaris missile-equipped submarines. More recently, the whole debate about the deployment of cruise missiles has passed the country by. Whatever the explanations offered for this, it seems that Turkey is not willing to allow its territory to be used for nuclear weapons in quite the way that the Federal Republic of Germany and the United Kingdom are.

During the 1970s, under the governments of Süleyman Demirel and Bülent Ecevit, Turkey appears to have made some strategically significant concessions to the Soviet Union. It seems that Soviet military jets were regularly allowed to overfly Turkey en route to Syria (although there were suggestions that this permission was withdrawn under the Ecevit government), and in 1976 the Soviet aircraft carrier, the *Kiev*, was allowed to travel through the Straits to the Mediterranean in what most external observers regarded as a clear breach of the terms of the 1936 Montreux Convention. This last event, of course, happened at a time when the US Congress had imposed an embargo on the sale of arms to Turkey.

Modernization of the Turkish armed forces has been another theme in the alliance. Turkey's army in the 1940s, described by the late Alastair Buchan as 'a form of outdoor relief', had progressed little beyond World War I in its levels of equipment. The equipment level of the Turkish armed forces has always depended on a trade-off between numbers and sophistication. Population growth since World War II, combined with an emphasis on conscription, has produced a long-term trend of a steady increase in numbers. During World War II the size of Turkey's armed forces rose almost tenfold, to 800,000 men, and was still around 700,000 when Turkey joined the alliance. During the 1950s, largely as a result of US advice, it was reduced to around 400,000 men. US instructors were brought in and service manuals translated into Turkish. A series of bilateral Turkish-American military agreements began, starting with the Military Facilities Agreement of June 1954 and continuing until the Defence and Economic Cooperation Agreement of March 1980.

Under the agreements, US troops and military installations began to operate on Turkish soil. At one point these involved about 24,000 officials and dependants. The present figure appears to be 5,000 or 6,000, according to Turkish officials. Since 1980 and the new DECA, the American military presence in Turkey has been subordinated to the Turkish structure: formally there are no longer any American bases, merely American personnel and equipment on Turkish bases. The functions of the American installations range from major airfields, such as İncirlik near Adana on the Mediterranean and Pırınçlık near Diyarbakır, to a number of scattered electronic and intelligence-gathering operations, some on a very small scale.

The role of intelligence-gathering in Turkey's relations with NATO and the USA appears to be considerable and has reportedly increased since the fall of Iran, though its extent can only be surmised. Its potential importance may be as potent a factor in determining Western thinking about Turkey as its current fruitfulness. Satellite communications may have reduced the need for land-based installations in countries bordering the Soviet Union, but the Turkish installations still appear to be very significant.

Turkey has taken a legalistic attitude towards the use of American military facilities on its soil for non-NATO purposes. In December 1983, the USA was permitted to use İncirlik as a stopping-off point for some troops moving into and out of the Lebanon. This was exceptional. In the various Arab-Israeli wars, different Turkish governments have showed great sensitivity to claims that the İncirlik base or another might be used to assist Israel directly or indirectly.

Since 1980 and the floating of the idea of a Rapid Deployment Force, Turkey has made it clear that it is not in favour of stationing troops of this kind on its soil. On the other hand, it has agreed on the modernization of a number of airfields, mostly in the east of the country at places such as Muş, Batman and Yüksekova. These increase the capacity of the Western alliance to intervene if, for example, there were to be a Soviet invasion of Iran. In general, however, the Turkish view of the role of NATO installations on its territory is that they are defensive rather than offensive. It does not want its carefully balanced relations with its neighbours, especially the Soviet Union, to be upset by anything which might create the impression that it would allow itself to be used as a bridgehead for military intervention by the alliance.

Another major consequence of Turkish membership of NATO has been a stream of military and economic aid intended to modernize the country's armed forces. Aid of this kind has in fact been under way since 1947 – before Turkish entry into NATO, In 1985 Turkey will receive more than $700m in aid from the USA, and expects to receive more than $1,000m in 1986. Turkey comes third in the list of recipients of US aid, after Israel and Egypt, and competes with both countries for it. The annual lobbying and skirmishing in the US Congress to get the administration's aid proposals accepted places major strains on Turkish-US relations and is described as 'nerve-racking' by Turkish officials, not least when the effort runs up against US Greek and Armenian (and sometimes pro-Israeli) lobbies trying to get the size of the package reduced.

The obligation to supply aid was written into the 1980 DECA, and it can be assumed that if US aid were permanently cut off, or reduced to negligible levels, there would be profound changes in Turkey's attitude towards the alliance. Indeed it is fairly clear that the style of Turkish military establishment since World War II has been the result of aid, a fact which is apparent again in the current moves to co-manufacture F-16 fighter jets in a joint venture with General Dynamics of the USA which fulfils a long-standing dream of the military leadership.

Complaints — well-founded — about the backwardness of the equipment of the Turkish military have to be set against a deliberate choice to maintain a conscript army which, at 600,000 men, remains much larger than that of any other NATO country outside the USA. It is at least arguable that a small and more expensively equipped fighting force would utilize a comparable amount of resources equally effectively. In Turkey, however, military service is regarded as an indispensable national tradition, essential to political and social cohesion.

NATO officials would probably prefer to see the annual doling out of aid by Congress, with all its political uncertainties, replaced by some kind of medium- or long-term funding arrangement intended to improve the fighting power of the Turkish armed forces. Most, however, would probably concede that this is politically and administratively impossible in the foreseeable future. While this is the case, Turkey's military importance to NATO will consist less in the capacity of its own forces than in the facilities afforded on its soil. Upgrading through NATO of the offensive military capacity of the Turkish armed forces would in any case provoke protests from Greece, and possibly one or two other members of the alliance, that it might be used as easily for regional as for NATO purposes.

The dispute with Greece has directly and indirectly bedevilled relations between the alliance and Turkey, even though the latter is usually regarded as a dutiful and reliable ally. American aid has to be pegged to a 7:10 ratio between Greece and Turkey, even when it has succeeded in passing through Congress. Disputes between the two erupt at NATO ministerial meetings and have forced Turkey and Greece to divert military resources away from their commitments to the alliance. They also of course provoked the estrangement of Greece from the alliance after 1974 and could conceivably some day do the same to Turkey.

Turkish officials report that even if Mr Papandreou's confrontational policies are poorly regarded in the West and viewed as unsuccessful, there is a strand of opinion inside Turkey which views Mr Papandreou's tactics as rewarding and advocates the use of 'blackmail' for political leverage. So far this school of thought has never gained the upper hand. The benefits to Turkey of the alliance make it unlikely that, barring a major upset with Greece, it would ever jeopardize its membership. As one of Turkey's few relatively neutralist foreign policy experts puts it, 'NATO is part of our culture'.

Membership of NATO goes well beyond simple military connections. As one American scholar puts it:

> Through her membership, Turkey was introduced to the circle of the American-West European political and diplomatic partnership. Consultation and discussion on a multilateral basis is generally more advantageous than bilateral contacts with a highly superior power. NATO membership allowed for a continuous and spontaneous exchange of views between Turkey and her collective allies. The value of such diplomatic contacts in political, economic and cultural relations is inestimable; more than anything else, it has enabled Turkey to establish herself as a 'European' power.[3]

Equally, a collective relationship with Turkey, whether inside NATO or the EC, often makes it easier for Western governments to deal with the country. On the other hand, the sense of community and political identity that stems from membership of an alliance is probably rather thin outside times of war. Turkey's membership of NATO creates in Turkish public opinion an expectation of psychological parity with the West which clashes with perceptions of relative economic backwardness and political isolation.

[3] Ferenc A. Vali, *Bridge Across the Bosporus* (Baltimore, Md., and London: Johns Hopkins Press, 1971), pp. 124–5.

6 European organizations

The Council of Europe

As with NATO, Turkey and Greece were latecomers to the Council of Europe, neither country being invited to its initial meeting in May 1949. The history of both countries' relations with the Council has subsequently raised problems which do not seem to have been encountered elsewhere.

Membership of the 21-member federation of European parliamentary democracies has major symbolic importance in both Turkey and Greece in establishing their European and democratic credentials. Inside the Council, however, the appearance of authoritarian governments in the two countries has created serious divisions, at both ministerial and, more particularly, parliamentary levels. These disagreements have never attracted very much attention in Western Europe because of the limited political significance there of the Council. For Turkey they have been important enough to attract regular press coverage and to colour its overall diplomatic and political relationship with West European countries. Can it be argued that the Council of Europe's dealings with Turkey illuminate the likely course of that country's relations within any future political association, such as the European Community?

An element of turning a blind eye has always been apparent in Turkey's relations with the Council. Western diplomats point out that the anti-communist provisions of the Turkish penal code, for example, are in theory a violation of the European Convention on Human Rights, and if Turkey were to be successfully prosecuted and expelled on that basis, it could not be readmitted to the Council while they remained in force.

In practice, however, the Council has tended to ignore the legal small print and focus on two types of issue. First, do member countries have freely elected, validly representative parliaments? Second, are major violations of human rights being carried out? In dealing with both these questions, the Council's attitude has been fluctuating and inconsistent, and it is evident that national political considerations and lobbying have generally prevailed. Thus, early in 1984, the Council voted to readmit a Turkish parliamentary delegation to its Parliamentary Assembly, even though the previous autumn the Assembly had voted that the general elections in Turkey would not represent a proper test of the popular will.

The debate inside the Council appears to be polarized between 'purists' (usually Socialists or Communists), who argue that conditions in Turkey fall short of those required for membership, and 'pragmatists', who claim that it will be easier to bring Turkish practices closer to European norms if the country is inside the Council. The degree of informedness on which such discussions are based appears to be very limited, and party-political attitudes are rigidly followed in most cases. Given that the Council is not regarded as a major international forum in Western Europe, the idea of making an exception for essentially diplomatic and strategic reasons does not appear to many of its members to be an unduly high price to pay.

Turkish attitudes towards the Council have traditionally been rather inflexible, with no variations of opinion between political parties being permitted to appear. It seems likely that Turkish governments regard the question of acceptability or otherwise in the Council as a matter of domestic as well as international prestige.

Late in 1984 when, largely as a result of several controversial human rights cases, the Council decided to delay Turkey's presidency of the Ministerial Council, the Özal government reacted angrily by threatening a walk-out. It had used a similar threat at the beginning of the year to get its parliamentary delegation accredited more swiftly than even Turkey's advocates in the Council had expected. Since the human rights cases (notably the prosecution of non-violent peace activists and Jehovah's Witnesses) appeared to raise serious questions about the similarity of Turkey's new form of parliamentary democracy to that of the Council members, it was not necessarily clear that the threat of a walk-out would always be the most effective diplomatic tactic.

In the longer term, tension-free membership of the Council will involve not merely a normalization of Turkey's human rights situation, but also a greater degree of like-mindedness. Whereas most European governments bring their legislation or administrative practices into line with the ruling of the European courts after a successful prosecution, Turkey regards any raising of its internal affairs in the European Court of Justice or the European Commission on Human Rights as intolerable interference. It remains one of the very few European countries which do not allow private citizens to raise cases in the European Court.

The feeling seems to be that Turkey's internal circumstances — and perhaps its isolated geopolitical situation — make it a special case. At press conferences, on several occasions, the present writer drew the attention of the Ulusu government to the fact that Britain accepted prosecution in the European Court by neighbouring governments and private individuals with equanimity and modified its legislation when required to do so. Was Turkey's attitude towards the European Court different and, if so, why? No answer was forthcoming. A very senior retired official, however, offers in private the answer that Turkey's conditions are so different from those of the rest of Europe that it has to be treated differently. This of course raises further awkward questions.

In longer-term perspective, despite its symbolic and secondary role, the Council of Europe has probably played a modest part in helping integrate Turkey into the mainstream of European life at the administrative level. Its role would probably have been greater had there been more feedback from successive Turkish parliamentary and official delegations about what they had seen and learned at Strasbourg. Public opinion inside Turkey does not seem to have been much educated by membership of the Council, despite the regular press coverage it receives. And this is not simply a consequence of censorship and unspoken taboos on discussion. All in all, Turkey's membership of the Council of Europe has proved an awkward precedent, and has generated controversies which may outweigh the rewards.

The European Community

In December 1984, Turkey celebrated the twentieth anniversary of the Treaty of Ankara, which established its Association Agreement with the

European Community. The celebrations were muted. The major provisions of the Association Agreement had not been working for half a decade. Its main committees had not met for several years. Diplomatic links between Turkey and the EC were at a fairly low ebb, with the prime minister singling out for criticism the Community's Ankara representative at briefings for the Turkish press. There was talk of an application for full membership of the Community, but this seemed to be simply part of a war of nerves with Brussels. In the opinion of most diplomatic observers in Ankara, the pro-European disposition in Turkey was waning. The minority who favoured an early Turkish application for full membership did so because they thought that if Turkey were incorporated in a 'political bloc' within Europe, it would be less likely to stray outside the Western orbit.

The possibility of an early application for full membership of the EC persists and would increase considerably if a government similar to Demirel's in 1980 were ever returned to power. European public opinion may well be taken by surprise, and at least some outright resistance to the principle of Turkey's full membership (although recognized in the Treaty of Ankara) is likely to emerge. In Brussels and Western capitals, the tendency over the past decade has been for politicians and officials to try to push the prospect of a Turkish application away to the political horizon. In Turkey, however, the idea of applying remains alive and unpredictable. EC officials have not begun to quantify the implications of Turkish full membership − nor indeed have Turkish ones. Some immediate results of a Turkish application (in contrast to Turkey's dealings with the Council of Europe) would be an increase in public interest in Turkey's internal affairs, greater press scrutiny of its credentials on human rights and democratic issues, and probably enhanced awareness of persisting social and cultural differences. These developments might be unacceptable to Turkey, particularly if they led to outright opposition to full membership and were accompanied by pressures from Community members that were regarded as hostile to Turkey.

The economic and fiscal problems for the Community and its institutions might in the longer term be insuperable. The precedents created by admitting peripheral states (from Britain to Greece), with economic bases divergent from those of the Community's original six members, are not very hopeful. But it is likely that Turkey will feel increasingly inclined to apply for membership, once Spain and Portugal are in the Community.

There is a strong case for an urgent and candid review by the Community of the future of its relationship with Turkey, and in particular an honest examination of its attitude to Turkish full membership and its likely implications. Simply postponing the issue will not make it go away, and may create a justifiable feeling inside Turkey that the Community has created expectations without intending to honour them.

Turkey's application for associate membership of the Community was made in July 1959. The move was in line with Turkish attempts to enter other Western economic bodies over the previous thirteen years. It took five years, however, before the association was formally set up and another nine years before the transitional period aimed at a customs union (envisaged for 1995) began. Turkey's moves towards the Community were modelled on similar ones by Greece. Unlike Greece, Turkey encountered a certain resistance to the idea that it was eligible to become a full member of the Community. Initial French hesitations on this point were eventually dispelled by Turkish lobbying in the form of a visit to the Elysée palace by the Turkish foreign minister of the day (1962-3).

Why did Turkey decide to set up an association aimed at full membership, rather than the more limited trade and aid arrangements which operated in other parts of the Mediterranean? Partly no doubt because of the example of Greece. Partly because the desire to 'enter Europe' was then at its peak in Turkey. Partly, possibly, because of its membership of NATO. This last element — not immediately or obviously relevant to Turkey's association agreement — is still regarded by some EC officials as the chief reason why Turkey gets different treatment from Tunisia or Israel in its dealings with the Community.

The implications of Turkish membership of the Community, if it happened, were slow to be grasped inside the country. A group of diplomats and elder statesmen from Turkey acted as lobbyists in the relationship between Turkey and the Community, propagating a European ideal which it is probably fair to say the majority of their compatriots neither shared nor knew about. For them, the idea of Turkey's eventual membership of the Community was the culmination of the westernization process that began with the Tanzimat period

(1839–76) in Turkey. In the 1960s, the Union of Chambers of Commerce conducted a study of the effects on Turkey of joining the Community or staying out of it, and concluded that it would make 'a possible gain or loss of about half a per cent of GNP'. In this spirit, during a period of semi-military rule when public opinion was relatively muzzled, the Community and Turkey went on to draw up terms for a programme of tariff cuts, culminating in a full customs union in 1995.

In a country where tariff barriers had been regarded as the cynosure of national independence for half a century, the programme of cuts was bound to excite criticism, and during the first half of the 1970s a fierce anti-Europeanism raged in the Turkish press. It was not confined to the centre and left in politics: the right-wing Nationalist Action Party and the ultra-religious National Salvation Party (of which at this date Mr Özal and his family were members) were both staunchly opposed to the EC, although the NAP seems later to have dropped its opposition. As a result, the treaty between the Community and Turkey confirming the 1973 enlargement of the EEC could not be placed before parliament for many years, and it was not until late in 1983 that it was ratified by the nominated Consultative Assembly.

Even in the early 1970s, however, it was obvious that Turkish political opinion, and in particular the opinion of industrialists (at that time a largely suspect new arrival on the national scene, who stood outside the political arena), was divided over the Community. There was a broad polarization between the 'forward-looking' industrialists of Istanbul, who controlled most of the large-scale manufacturing and were interested in penetrating export markets, and smaller-scale producers in Anatolia, who supplied traditional domestic markets. Meanwhile the programme of cuts, organized into two lists, became harder and harder to apply. In 1977 the government stopped making the annual tariff reductions on EC imports, and since then there has been no progress on the Turkish side towards a customs union.

At the same time, Turkish industrialists and politicians were fighting vigorously to obtain easier terms for the entry of Turkish products into the Community. In the late 1970s the Community was induced to ease restrictions on some Turkish agricultural exports, after Turkey had drawn attention to the superior terms being offered to Israel and countries in the Maghrib. There has also been a protracted battle over

Turkish textile exports to the Community, notably cotton yarn, T-shirts and towelling. Here the interests of Turkish industry have been pitched against those of declining industries in Western Europe. There is a faint parallel to the 'infant industry' arguments which were used in Turkey to justify high tariff barriers against EC imports, but such a parallel finds no sympathizers in Turkey. It is not unfair to say that there is indignation at the fact that Europe does not practise the free-trade policies it preaches.

The Community has not proved much of a match for vigorous opposition of this kind. By various means, including exporting through third countries such as Greece, the quotas that it has imposed on Turkish textile exports have been generally rendered meaningless, and the battle – which at one stage led to Turkey's imposing a retaliatory levy of 15 per cent on EC iron and steel and polystyrene imports – has fizzled out. Turkey's situation as a relatively large producer on the edge of the Community is, however, bound to produce strains from time to time. During 1984, for example, Greek attempts to introduce an MIP – minimum import price – for imports of figs and sultanas threatened to rob traditional Turkish producers of their livelihood, although curiously this did not find its way into the Turkish press.

By the early 1980s, however, the architects of Turkish-EC relations were having to grapple with very much larger problems. The institutional framework devised for the association agreement had not withstood the test of time. Changes in Turkey and in the Community had produced an exasperating stalemate in political as well as in economic relations.

When Greece announced in 1975 that it would apply for full membership of the Community at an early date, Turkey paid little attention: possibly because of the prevailing climate of anti-EC feeling and widespread doubts about the feasibility of a customs union. Hints from some Western parliamentarians that Turkey should immediately lodge its own application were ignored. It was some five years later that the ultra-European foreign minister of the Demirel minority government, Hayrettin Erkmen, announced that Turkey would be applying for full membership at an early date, probably before the end of 1980. In fact, by September of that year, he had been uniquely deposed from office by parliament, and a week later the military had intervened in Turkey's political life for the sixth time this century, thus ruling out any chance of an application for full membership for some years. The prospect of such an application at an early date might have sent shudders through officials in Brussels. In fact the suggestion seems to have been widely regarded as being so preposterous that it would have been treated only as a diplomatic ploy.

Turkish candidature for the EC raises very large questions which many in Europe often prefer to treat as unrealistic or simply to ignore. Turkey's land area is exactly half that of the old Nine, before the accession of Greece. Its population at present would make it rank fifth in the Community, but by the end of the century it will be larger than any Community state except a reunited Germany. There are the obvious cultural differences which are far stronger than those between, say, Portugal and the Community; moreover, Turkey, apart from its small border with Greece, will never be contiguous with the rest of the EC. It is considerably poorer than any of the other Mediterranean countries that are joining the Community: by the early 1980s per capita GNP in Turkey was back below the $1,000 mark. The implications for the regional or social funds of the Community are literally unthinkable, unless membership is treated simply in terms of being part of a 'political bloc'. As a Turkish diplomat in a Western capital wrily observes, 'Turkey will never be ready for membership of the European Community, because by the time it is, the European Community will have ceased to exist.'

Against this, Turkey is well placed to argue that the Community has already embarked upon a substantial departure from its original principles in admitting Greece, Spain and Portugal. The difference involved as far as Turkey is concerned is simply one of degree. None of this seems to have been perceived in Turkey, where relations with the Community are still largely seen in terms of David and Goliath. The implications for Turkey, favourable as well as unfavourable, of Greek accession are rarely discussed. Turkey has also signally failed to alert itself to the forthcoming consequences of the Spanish and Portuguese accessions, and could yet face a Greek/Spanish/Portuguese alliance against it as a result.

In fact Turkish-EC relations are still seen in Ankara in bilateral terms. This is probably partly an unintended consequence of the establishment in the early 1970s of an EC Information Office in Ankara, which has helped not only to defuse the anti-European current in the Turkish press of a decade ago, but to sharpen Turkish bureaucratic perceptions of the Community as a political *lusus naturae* of whose activities it can make little sense.

This perception derives largely from the fact that the political ground rules of the Community, as embodied in the Treaty of Rome and subsequent legislation, impose certain scrutineering functions upon it which do not exist for a unitary national state. At one level this is seen most starkly in the dilemma of EC officials in Ankara who, having to report debates in the European Parliament in their official local-language magazine, are at a loss to know what to do about speeches from communist members which would be published routinely elsewhere in Europe but in Turkey are, at least technically, indictable. At another level, it is discernible in the freezing of economic aid worth $530m due to Turkey under the Fourth Financial Protocol since 1981.

It is sometimes argued that the attitudes of the Community towards Turkey are more complex than those of individual European governments because of differences between its recruiting procedures and those of national civil services. It seems more likely that the Commission is having to face questions which also trouble the Council of Europe, questions which would be given increasing prominence if Turkey were to become more closely involved in West European institutions.

Most of these difficulties are to do with human rights. Since the early 1970s this has been an area in which divergences between European and North American attitudes have been conspicuous, with the latter showing a tendency to present European concern on human rights issues in Turkey as an interference in the country's internal affairs. From the European point of view, there are explicit legal obligations against which standards have to be measured, and one of the purposes of the Community's existence is to avoid a return to the conflicts and lapses in civilized standards which upset the life of the Continent before 1945. The doctrine of 'Turkish exceptionalism' is thus more likely to create a predisposition to exclude Turkey from Europe than to secure its admission on privileged terms. To Western diplomats who have to try to bridge the gap between public opinion in their own countries and the situation as seen in Ankara, many of the controversial human rights problems since 1980 in Turkey almost seem to have been created with a view to straining relations with Brussels to the uttermost. How else can one explain the gaoling of the 30 members of the Executive Committee of the Turkish Peace Association; the torture of the former mayor of Istanbul, Ahmet İsvan; the holding of trade unionists in prison for up to four years; the five-year gaol sentences for Jehovah's Witnesses; the sustained harassment of the Turkish correspondent of an American news agency; the indictment of intellectuals for organizing a petition to President Evren; and many other cases? These events have all followed high-level political choices in Turkey.

In Brussels, it seems to be assumed that Turkey's leadership is well aware of the unfeasibility of an early application for full membership. Preoccupied with the likely consequences of the Spanish and Portuguese enlargement, EC officials believe that the priorities as far as Turkey is concerned are (1) to improve the political relationship – which will depend on some gestures from the Turkish side; (2) to reactivate the association agreement and hold meetings of the organs of the association, the Turkey-EEC Joint Parliamentary Association Council in particular; and (3) to restore the flow of aid blocked since 1981.

In Turkey, Mr Özal's government follows its predecessors in suggesting that an application for full membership may be close, and the prime minister has sometimes spoken of a 'surprise application' – as if it, or the threat of it, were part of a diplomatic game of cat-and-mouse rather than the natural outcome of historical and economic affinities. Equally, Turkey's attempts to reactivate the Joint Parliamentary Association Council have tended to try and force the pace of developments in a way which has caused at least some members of the European Parliament to question the motivation behind them. The underlying spirit of Turkish-EC relations in the mid-1980s is thus tense and not very happy.

Although the consequences of an early application for full membership have been spelt out to Ankara – embarrassing political isolation and possibly two vetoes – it is by no means clear that the top leadership, possibly on US advice, will decide that such an application is the wrong way forward. The Community appears to be hoping for a breathing-space of about a decade before an application is made, by which time it is hoped that convergence between Turkey's economic and political systems and those of the Community member states will have made the choice much easier. The trends of the past decade, however, unfortunately suggest that problems could as easily multiply as diminish.

For this reason some Community officials argue for the need to draw Turkey more actively into the mainstream of European life by separating technical progress from political issues. This would mean more concentration on joint efforts in research and development, standards, the elimination of technical barriers, and the work of official and professional bodies including trade unions and employers' organizations. Turkey could play a much more active role in European food industries' organizations or textile bodies and other lobby groups. All this would seem to imply an effort from Europe, since the knowledge on which to base such contacts is largely lacking inside Turkey.

In the meantime Turkey will probably continue to send about 35 to 40 per cent of its exports to the Community and to purchase a steady 28 per cent of its imports from the Ten. In 1984 Turkey's trade deficit with the Community narrowed significantly, and export orientation seems bound to stimulate further the long-standing interest of Turkish industrialists in the Community. It is conceivable that Turkey might choose a 'Korean option' and plump for moderate isolation. Given the strong emotional, historical and cultural elements in the relationship, however, the future is more likely to be one of unresolved and largely misunderstood tensions and disputes.

7 Some bilateral problems

The preceding sections have contained a number of recurrent leitmotifs about Turkish-Western relations, which it may be worth looking at more closely. The limited press coverage of Turkey means that some persistent and increasingly serious problems – the quarrel with France, for example – are virtually unknown outside the country, while others, such as the presence of Turkish migrant workers in Western Europe, are not usually looked at in the overall context of Turkish relations with the West.

Historical prejudice

Turks living in Western Europe consistently – though not vociferously – complain of an undercurrent of hostility in public opinion, often based not on attitudes to individuals but on stereotyped historical prejudices. Similar complaints, of course, are to be heard from nationals of other peripheral countries (including Greece), and the way in which public opinion and self-images are managed in Turkey means that a certain degree of ego-bruising may be inevitable when citizens of a relatively closed world are exposed to one in which there are fewer restrictions on the range of expression. Tests of public opinion seem, however, to confirm the idea that Turks are regarded with more antipathy than, say, Italians or Greeks. In several of the countries of continental Europe, perceptions of Turkey are complicated by attitudes to mass immigration. Elsewhere it seems that attitudes are partly conditioned by the centuries of antagonism between the Ottoman Empire and Europe. Consider, for example, the following passage in a survey of early modern Europe:

The Ottoman State, occupant of South-Eastern Europe for five hundred years, camped in the continent without ever becoming naturalized into its social or political system. It always remained largely a stranger to European culture, as an Islamic intrusion into Christendom, and has posed intractable problems of presentation to unitary histories of the continent to this day . . . From the Renaissance onwards, indeed, European political thinkers in the age of Absolutism repeatedly sought to define the character of their own world by opposition with that of the Turkish order, so close and yet so remote from it; none of them reduced the distance simply or mainly to one of religion.[4]

It seems important that Turkish-Western relations — and more particularly Turkish-West European relations — be future-oriented if they are to have much chance of prospering. In the long run, the conquest of prejudice probably depends on the success of Turkish industrialization and the change in national image which would follow this. In the short term, historical prejudices may not be as important a handicap as many Turks appear to feel they are. In Britain, at least, migrant Turks seem to be able to adjust relatively easily to their new environment, and in another Anglo-Saxon environment, the United States, the Turkish community is actually elitist, professional and highly successful — the opposite of its counterparts in the Netherlands and West Germany. To some extent, the Turkish authorities themselves probably impede the improvement of their country's image by making it difficult for Western graduate scholars to conduct research in Turkey (access to archives and libraries is notoriously difficult) which would result in books about the country. Equally, the attempt to combat historical prejudices — which is legitimate — can sometimes be confused with efforts to impose a particular historical interpretation which may be at variance with the facts as understood in the West.

Turkey's image in the West would obviously also be improved if the country made a stronger international showing in sport and the arts. Its weak record in sport is largely attributable to lack of investment in training and facilities in schools. As far as the arts are concerned, we seem to have stumbled on another of the contrasts between Turkish

[4] Perry Anderson, *Lineages of the Absolutist State* (London: New Left Books, 1974), p. 397.

and Western societies. The bureaucracy dominates much of the performing arts, while those that are not in effect under a degree of state patronage and control are starved of funds and prestige, and suffer from the antagonism between the State and intellectuals. The only two Turkish cultural figures who have made much impact outside the country in the twentieth century are the Communist Expressionist poet, Nazim Hikmet, who has been given a place in the cultural pantheon of the Eastern bloc, and the pro-Albanian Marxist film director Yılmaz Güney. Efforts to promote 'approved' cultural contacts have not until recently been particularly numerous, and seem hardly likely to acquire much vitality. Again, the reassertion of Islamic traditionalism may complicate matters. In the Turkey of the 1980s, one from time to time reads newspaper articles urging that the attention of Western tourists in the country be directed away from Graeco-Roman ruins and focused on Turkish Islamic civilization.

Nationalism versus pluralism

As long as the maintenance of authority and a stable national identity are felt to be problem areas by Turkish governments, it seems likely that there will be at least a potential conflict with European and Western public opinion, especially over attitudes towards ethnic, religious and other minorities. Indeed, Turkish officials sometimes surprise their European colleagues in discussions of minority problems in forums such as the Council of Europe by claiming that there are no minorities in Turkey. Given the increasingly international and activist behaviour of many minority rights groups, it is virtually certain that from time to time these will clash with the Turkish authorities. Such clashes are likely to become much more frequent if Turkey involves itself more with the West. Already Kurdish groups inside Turkey have substantial support from sympathizers in the Netherlands, West Germany and Scandinavia. In trying to contain the forces of disruption in the south-east of the country, the Turkish authorities can plausibly claim that their policies are the only alternative to a general upheaval and much loss of life. On the other hand, the same argument seems less effective when applied to press and book censorship or to some curbs on the freedom of association. Finally, cases such as the five years' gaoling of 23 Jehovah's Witnesses, or a certain reluctance to accept the logical implication of pluralism that atheism or non-Muslim religions should be socially acceptable, suggest that, as elsewhere in the Middle East, religion is still a major component of national identity and that there is little likelihood of Turkey becoming pluralist in this respect in the near future.

Economic and social development may soften this picture, and help to integrate society and blur the contrast between primordial group-ings. Or it may not. Urbanization in Central Anatolia in the 1960s and 1970s politicized the long-standing but not very explicit antagonism between Alevis and Sunnis, and split the towns of Çorum, Sivas and Kahramanmaraş into warring suburbs in which murder threatened to divide the population as finally as in Nicosia, Beirut or Jerusalem. Against this has to be set the broad success of the Turkish Republic's conscious policy of cultural assimilation since the 1920s.

In the long term an industrialized Turkey may evolve in the direc-tion of pluralism as it is understood in the West. In the meantime there is a strong probability that greater familiarity will lead to more collisions between Turkish ways of doing things and Western public opinion, even under, for example, a centre-left government. As Turkish expatriate groups in Western Europe go into their second and third generations, it is quite possible that — as with Greek and Spanish emigrants — they will increasingly develop political lobby groups and that there will be more debate about internal affairs in Turkey. So far Europe seems to have responded to such issues by making a tacit exception for Turkey because of its strategic importance. But Western diplomats, who have the un-comfortable role of trying to cushion possible collisions, are aware that public opinion will not necessarily remain relatively dormant — it was, after all, far from dormant during the nineteenth century, at a time when Turkey was a strategic ally of England.

Turkish communities abroad

Until the late 1950s, the number of Turks who had travelled outside their country this century was too small to make any impact on the consciousness of the West. During the 1960s and for the first few years of the 1970s (until the recession in Western Europe halted the process), about two million Turks migrated in search of work abroad, going to destinations as widely scattered as Australia, Israel, Libya, Britain, Saudi Arabia, Scandinavia and, of course, West Germany. For the first time, Turks became a visible presence in Western Europe, making the kebab almost as familiar as the hamburger in big cities, and introducing Turkish newspapers to news-stands. To some extent European attitudes towards Turkey and the Turks began to be based on direct personal contact.

As individuals, Turks seem to have no difficulty in establishing themselves in a West European setting. The image of all Turks encountered by British acquaintances of the present writer in the United Kingdom, for example, seems without exception to be favourable. On the other hand, when Turkish groups and communities are involved, especially in continental Europe, the picture seems to be rather different.

The most basic problem appears to be that the social and cultural gap between middle-class Turkish families and workers is still sufficiently great to hinder the adaptation of the latter to European life. While Turkish students, doctors, engineers, architects and professional people quickly merge into a European background, recently arrived peasants from remote Anatolian villages cannot do so. Furthermore, the Turkish middle class in continental Europe seems to have been much less successful than its Indian and Pakistani counterparts in Britain in supplying communal leadership or mediating between lower-class immigrants and the host society. There is a striking lack of identifiable Turkish community leaders in West Germany which is otherwise hard to explain. Outside civil society in many respects, lower-class migrants — exhorted constantly by the Turkish press not to lose their language and their Turkishness — have reacted by turning inwards and in some cases becoming more Islamic than might have been the case had they stayed in Turkey. Officials of some host countries complain that the Turkish authorities have insisted on sending in religious officials (from a secular state) who further complicate such matters as the education of girls in mixed schools and other aspects of integration in a modern post-religious society.

Sometimes lower-class Turks have proved fertile ground for conversion to Marxism. It may have been this extreme form of politicization that was responsible for the breakdown in relations between Turkish workers and the surrounding community in the Netherlands during the 1970s, when there were race riots. In 1984 two Turkish workers were murdered in racial violence in France, and even in Britain the National Front seems to cast a shadow across an otherwise much happier picture.

By the early 1980s, the West German government, which had always regarded foreign immigration as a temporary rather than an irreversible event, was committed to policies of assisted repatriation. *Fremdenhass*, hatred of foreigners, had become a catchword in Turkish newspapers, and a steady stream of Turks (estimated to rise to about 300,000 by the end of 1985) was returning from West Germany.

The history of the Turkish community in West Germany is only a quarter of a century old, and even with assisted repatriation schemes the number of Turks in the country is unlikely to fall below the million mark. It is hard to predict future developments, but Turks in the Federal Republic speak of a remarkable sense of insecurity. The failure so far of the Turkish-West German relationship has distanced Turkey from the European power which is its chief trade partner in the OECD area and has been its main diplomatic ally since World War II. West Germany has also been a major supplier of military and economic aid. Turkey receives a larger proportion (7.5 per cent) of the Federal Republic's overseas development assistance than any other country. None the less, there is a lack of popular interest in Turkey, as shown, for example, by the paucity of full-time permanent German correspondents in the country.

Despite this there is a certain amount of interaction. Turkish political conflicts of the pre-1980 period continue to be fought out, sometimes literally, in West Germany and to a lesser extent in other European countries. Events such as the suicide of a Turkish leftist, who feared forcible repatriation to Turkey, and the brief demonstration in Ankara in the spring of 1984 by a group of Greens of the Bundestag suggest that the presence of a Turkish minority in Western Europe will continue to have spill-over effects. The experience of Turkish workers in Western Europe has shown that they can become a skilled and diligent industrial workforce — something which in the early 1960s had not yet been demonstrated on a large scale inside Turkey. Apart from this, it is difficult to draw many encouraging lessons for the short term from the experience of Turkish migrant workers in Western Europe. So far there seems to have been remarkably little cultural cross-fertilization, and in some West German cities, at least, working-class Turkish families seem to have reacted against their new environment by becoming overtly Islamic and anti-Western.

Turkey and France

Relations between Turkey and West Germany have remained business-like throughout the strains of the last decade. By contrast, relations between Turkey and France have become so unfriendly that France is the only country (even including the Soviet Union) which Turkish officials actually name in private as unfriendly, and the ordinary Turk in the street is perhaps more likely to express indignation at France than he is at Greece. The development is a recent one and is largely linked with the Armenian terrorist campaign against Turkish diplomats. Before the 1970s, Turkey and France had a long-standing cultural alliance stretching back into the last century, and the influence of French on the Turkish had been greater than that of any other European language. The roots of the quarrel lie in a number of relatively small episodes: the presence of a French cabinet minister at a ceremony in 1973 at which a plaque was unveiled to victims of an alleged Turkish genocide of Armenians during World War I; remarks by French cabinet ministers (notably the present French minister of defence) apparently condoning the assassinations of Turkish diplomats; the leniency of French courts towards Armenians accused of involvement in terrorist activities; and media coverage of the murders (more of which have happened in Paris than in any other city).

Turkey has responded with sustained press criticism of France, demonstrations outside the French Embassy (the only ones permitted in the country since 1980) and an informal trade boycott which has at times brought it into conflict with the European Commission. The lobbying for the Airbus 310-A during the summer of 1984 had to be organized so as to present it as a predominantly West German venture, with France's role in it being played down. The advent of President Mitterrand was hailed in Turkey as an opportunity for an improvement in relations. In fact the deterioration has continued, and a visit to

Ankara in July 1984 by a special emissary of President Mitterrand seems to have had little effect.

What is the reason for this dispute, which has contributed considerably to Turkey's isolation from Western Europe since 1980? The existence of a large Armenian minority in France is usually identified by Turks as the main cause. Other factors may be France's relatively detached position inside the Atlantic Alliance and at least two decades of alignment with Greece.

For Turkey, the dispute has enlarged the number of potential opponents it has to contend with in the Council of Europe and the European Parliament. It has also added a major European power to the five minor countries prosecuting it in the European Court of Justice. It has made any progress towards full membership of the European Community very much harder: French officials have in the past been heard to question Turkey's credentials as a European state (though others argue that the 1964 Treaty of Ankara, which allowed for eventual full membership, settles this question), and even if there is not a French veto on a Turkish application, the opposition of France will reinforce that of Turkey's more predictable enemies.

More generally, the dispute with France indicates what might happen if Turkey's strategic importance ceased to be regarded as indispensable, and hostile public opinion began to play a major part in determining government policy in other Western countries. Successive Turkish governments have not found ways of coping with this situation other than to express outrage through the media at home, and to try to bring diplomatic pressure to bear via other Western countries.

Eastern Europe

Since the end of World War II, most of Turkey's East European neighbours have been communist states in the Soviet camp. There is little doubt that Turkey's credibility as a European nation would look greater if the Iron Curtain countries were free to play their own roles in a noncommunist Europe. Although it has somewhat diminished, Turkey's interest in its relations with the Balkan countries continues to be strong, not least because of its rivalry with Greece, which affects the others as well. Moreover, the similarity of the bureaucratic state apparatus in

East bloc countries makes it easier, in some respects, for Turkey to have cultural exchanges with them than with the West.

Turkey, Romania and Bulgaria have a common interest in protecting the international waterways in the Aegean, and Bulgaria and Romania are both important to the Turkish economy: Bulgaria because it has, for a decade, been supplying electricity from its national grid to meet the needs of Turkish Thrace (under an arrangement that was originally intended to be reciprocal and temporary), and Romania as a major supplier of project aid. Romania's largest project in Turkey to date is the Fourth Turkish Refinery at Kırıkkale, now nearing completion.

Political relations with the Balkan countries are usually shrouded in obscurity, but despite tensions between Turkey and Bulgaria, there has been an exchange of visits by Presidents Evren and Zhivkov to each other's capitals during the last three years. Indeed President Evren visited Bulgaria before any other European country and followed it with trips to Yugoslavia and Romania. The visit to Bulgaria, in February 1982, was intended to bury differences between Turkey and that country over Bulgaria's efforts to 'destabilize' Turkey by channelling weapons into it before 1980. This and a series of minor espionage scandals continue to cause problems, but Turkey seems to find it fairly easy to deal with Bulgaria (the Bulgarian foreign minister, Peter Mladenov, visited Ankara in July 1984), or did so before early 1985.

Yugoslavia traditionally counts as one of Turkey's warmest friends and, exceptionally, the existence of Turkish and Muslim minorities within its borders acts as a bond between the two countries. By contrast, the approximately 10 per cent of the Bulgarian population which is Turkish is a source of friction. Large numbers of Turks, born either in Yugoslavia or Bulgaria, have subsequently settled in Turkey. Early in 1985, there was a flare-up in relations between the Bulgarian government and the Bulgarian Turkish minority, apparently as a result of a forcible slavicization policy intended to reduce the number of Muslim Turks. There were unconfirmed reports that as many as 400 or 500 ethnic Turks might have been killed in clashes. The Turkish government reacted pragmatically to what was apparently a more severe outbreak of violence than any in Cyprus since 1954, when relations between Turkish and Greek Cypriots began to break down. Turkish press response was certainly less strident than would have been the case for a similar incident involving Turks in Greece or any other Western country. It appears that, despite the uneasiness of public opinion (often cited as an insuperable block to certain conciliatory moves in Cyprus), Turkey felt that it could not afford a confrontation with Bulgaria, both because of its backing by a hostile great power and because of common economic interests.

Turkey and Yugoslavia, along with Greece, were parties to an alliance – the Balkan Pact – in 1954 which was quickly abandoned because of improved relations between Yugoslavia and the Soviet Union and tensions between Greece and Turkey over Cyprus. As long as Soviet hegemony persists in most of the Balkans, the scope for regional co-operation of any kind with Turkey will be limited, but the area is traditionally one with which Turkey has strong links and in which Turkish diplomacy seems rather more self-assured than it is in Western Europe.

Even if there were a politically fluid situation in the region, however, it is unlikely that Eastern Europe would form an alternative pole of attraction for Turkey in the way in which, to some extent, the Islamic world does. More probably, as in the pre-1939 period, the politics of the region would mirror the divisions among the great powers, and this would determine Turkey's relations with particular countries.

8 Turkey and the Western financial system

Official institutions

After World War II, foreign aid became a major factor in Turkish economic development, even though the reliance on high tariff barriers and self-sufficiency continued. As a result the country joined, and has remained a member of, the major Western international economic agencies. It became a member of the International Bank for Reconstruction and Development and the International Monetary Fund in 1947, and it was a founder member of both the Organization for European Economic Cooperation and the European Payments Union in 1948.

Early in 1954, the government also introduced legislation that was intended to attract foreign capital into the country, notably Law 6224. The subsequent inflow of funds was not very impressive – $35m by the end of 1959 – but it was an improvement on the $6m during the preceding four years. Meanwhile Turkey continued to run deficits on its balance of trade and on the current account, while maintaining a fixed exchange rate. During the 1948–59 period the country received $1,210m of economic aid from the United States, of which 58 per cent was grants in aid. The amount of US military aid was presumably larger.

The acute mismanagement of the Turkish economy at many points from the 1950s to the 1970s forced Western donor countries, particularly the United States and the Federal Republic of Germany, to take action. Throughout the period, in order to avoid inflaming national sensibilities, pressure to change economic policies was usually exerted through the international agencies such as the IMF and, in the devaluation operation of 1958, the European Payments Union. For much of the period before 1980, however, cooperation between the government of the day in Ankara and the IMF was usually grudging and minimal, and there were long spells when the dialogue was broken off.

The depressing picture of high inflation, severe budgetary and trade deficits, and chaotic indebtedness made most European governments reluctant to extend substantial economic aid. 'There appear to have been doubts about Turkey's ability to carry out a rational debt management programme,' writes one author, speaking of the early 1960s, 'much less embark upon a systematic development effort.'[5] As a result, in 1962 the OECD set up a consortium for aid to Turkey, through which most governmental aid from the West was channelled. During the seven years up to 1970, net aid from the West amounted to only $1,160m in total, and the flow of foreign investment, at a time when most of the major subsidiaries of international companies now operating in Turkey were being set up, was a mere trickle: a net private capital inflow of $51m by 1969, with net outflows of capital in most years. The IMF and the OECD supplied recommendations which appear to have formed the basis for the August 1970 devaluation and stabilization operation, just as they had done twelve years earlier in the 1958 crisis, and as they would do again in the 1980 Stabilization Programme.

Although it was established that, in the last resort, Turkey would listen to international advice, the climate was a depressing one for potential foreign investors, who had to contend with a hostile bureaucracy and public opinion. 'The Turks were left with the reputation of being ever recalcitrant in the economic field and hence willing to conform to the wisdom of the world's economists only *in extremis*,' writes one American scholar of the 1958 crisis.[6] His words apply even more forcefully to the chaotic mismanagement of the economy between 1975 and 1979, and particularly to the years 1975–7. During this period, state-regulated prices, including those of imported fuels, were held down whenever it was possible to do so, fixed and unrealistic exchange rates were maintained and, before the flow of funds dried up in April 1977, about $2.3bn was borrowed on the Eurodollar markets in short-term money to finance imports. This situation may have been

[5] Anne O. Krueger, *Foreign Trade Regimes and Economic Development: Turkey* (New York and London: Columbia U.P., 1974), p. 133.
[6] George S. Harris, *Troubled Alliance: Turkish-American Problems in Historical Perspective, 1945–1971* (Washington D.C.: American Enterprise Institute for Public Policy Research, 1972), p. 75.

partly a reflection of Turkey's geopolitical importance. Whereas outside observers explain the inflow of funds from private banks during 1975-7 in terms of government guarantees and high rates of return, some of the banks themselves attribute it to 'political pressures'.

By the end of 1979, the situation was sufficiently alarming to be extensively discussed at the Guadeloupe summit of Western leaders, and the OECD Consortium was being wound up for a new rescue programme. Despite the severity of the economic crisis in Turkey in early 1980, when heat and light were frequently unavailable during a bad winter, Turkish assumptions that in the last resort the country would always be 'bailed out' by the Western world seem to have been borne out by events.

The 1980 crisis, however, had much longer-lasting effects on the relations between Turkey and the international agencies than its predecessors. For the following three years, the OECD Consortium had to put up annual amounts of $1,000m in assistance to Turkey. A three-year Stand-By Agreement (at the suggestion of the new policy-makers in Ankara) was signed with the IMF in June 1980. Turkey became a model country as far as the Fund and the World Bank were concerned, and was the major beneficiary of the World Bank's Structural Adjustment Loan programme in five tranches up to 1984.

For the first time, the international agencies began to assume a degree of responsibility, at least indirectly, for mistakes in Turkish economic policy. It seems, for example, that the decision to free interest rates completely in July 1980 and the jolts to the financial system which followed, culminating in the crashes of late 1981 and June–July 1982, were prompted by advice from the IMF. There seems to have been some private discussion inside the international agencies about the degree to which Turkey's internal structure was fully understood by those prescribing its medicine and whether further mishaps might not follow. The Fund, for its part, felt sufficiently committed to the Turkish experiment to keep extremely quiet in 1983 when it was revealed that the then Turkish finance minister had doctored statistics showing the growth of currency in circulation.

Despite the very close relationship which seems to prevail at present between the international agencies and the Ozal government, it is clear that any Turkish government will always be somewhat more committed to fast-growth policies than to bringing the current account into equilibrium. During late 1984, Turkish officials indicated that the fairly ambitious growth targets of the newly announced Fifth Five-Year Plan had been obliquely criticized by the Fund, which had produced two alternative five-year scenarios, trading off slower growth against an improved current account performance. Turkey's social and demographic problems mean that any Turkish government will always opt for GNP growth of at least 5 to 7 per cent. Turkish governments are also likely to press the Western world to assume as much as possible of the burden of financing the 600,000-strong Turkish army, in order to minimize the degree to which defence spending acts as a brake on economic development.

Private institutions

A few foreign companies in Turkey, notably insurance companies, go back more than a hundred years. One or two foreign investors, for instance the Nestlé Company, can trace their presence in the country back before 1914. For the most part, however, until after World War II, Turkey was effectively insulated from the international banking and business community. Even up to 1980, the majority of foreign investment in the country (totalling less than $500m) was there essentially to secure a long-term foothold in the market. Bureaucratic obstacles, payment delays, restrictions on foreign personnel (and the absence of local facilities for their families), a discriminatory tax system, and the failure to apply foreign investment incentives deterred all but the most determined investors. A number of foreign companies actually pulled out of Turkey during the late 1970s.

Since 1980, however, new legislation designed to ease the lot of existing foreign investors and attract new ones has been passed. The glaring anomalies which, for example, barred the Nestlé Company from repatriating any of its profits after the mid-1960s, so that it had to deposit them with the Central Bank and borrow them back at interest, have now been eliminated. A Foreign Investment Department with powers to approve most investments under $50m has been set up, and many restrictions, including some on importing raw materials, have been loosened. Despite this, the inflow of foreign investment into

Turkey has been disappointing so far. The actual amount of new money coming into the country has been much less than the figures given for investments authorized by the government and is usually well below $100m a year. It is estimated that $45m flowed in during the first six months of 1984, for instance, whereas official figures claimed authorizations of around $350m.

Many Western firms still apparently prefer licensing agreements to joint ventures as far as Turkey is concerned. If present policies continue, however, the second half of the 1980s is likely to see a steady increase in the volume of direct private investment and a revival of Turkish private-sector investment. The most critical question for foreign investors will be whether the Ozal government can manage to bring down inflation and hold it permanently at 25 per cent or below.

The harbingers of change have been banks and financial institutions. American Express and Citibank had already decided to come into Turkey in the late 1970s, before the policy turnaround had come over the horizon. The number of foreign banks has risen from four to fifteen, and they have been followed by five major international accounting groups. Turkey is thus beginning to show up on the international financial maps in a way it did not do a decade ago. Although foreign banks have found it very easy to make large profits on their branches in Turkey (American Express, for example, made $7m on its Istanbul branch in 1983) and are sensitive to any possible rivalry with Turkey's inefficient domestic banking sector, there has not been any parallel to date with the economic xenophobia which was widespread in the 1960s.

A further indication of the internationalization of the Turkish financial sector is the increasing number of Turkish banks that now operate branches and representative offices in Western Europe, the Gulf and North America. During 1984, permission was also given to two Islamic banks, officially described as 'private financial institutions', to set up in Turkey. The Al Baraka Investment and Development Company of Saudi Arabia set up a $13m venture, the Al Baraka Türk Özel Finans Kurumu AS, with Hak Yatırım, a firm owned by the prime minister's brother, Mr Korkut Özal. The Faisal Finans Kurumu is a second such venture: 90 per cent is owned by the Faisal Islamic Bank, the Dar al Maal al Islami, and other partners from Saudi Arabia, the Bahamas, Egypt and Bahrein; and the Turkish 10 per cent of its $13m capital comes from two members of the dissolved National Salvation Party, Mr Salih Özcan and Mr Ahmet Tevfik Paksu.

At present the internationalization of the Turkish business world is still essentially in its first generation, with most of the major trading houses dating back less than a decade and with the number of bankers with international expertise and training probably fewer than fifty. English has already, however, become a lingua franca in Istanbul's Büyükdere Caddesi, the main headquarters of the country's industry, and it is hard to find a Turkish corporation of any size which does not now do at least some export business.

Although exchange-rate policy remains the critical factor – the government is committed not only to maintaining realistic exchange rates but also to gradual progress towards full convertibility of the Turkish lira – as far as the future of the export drive is concerned, it is hard to imagine Turkey returning to the policies of the 1970s. Even those industrialists who want a more gradual depreciation of the lira are careful to stress that they do not expect to see a return to fixed exchange rates.

The opening up of the economy to the outside world, which appears to have popular support, has entailed a cautious liberalization of import policies, with foreign consumer goods now being available to Turks in ordinary grocers shops, subject to a stiff surcharge. Turkey's role as a trading nation is likely to increase, and although the markets in the Middle East will continue to be vital to the country's fortunes, this should, on balance, mean increasing westernization in terms of patterns of consumption and life-style. It is also likely, though less certain, to mean more Europeanization: Turkish consumers at present look to Europe for some products, but more often styles and taste can be surprisingly closely linked with those of the United States.

The history of Turkey's economic policies over the past three decades is one of alternating profligacy and retrenchment as far as its relations with the creditor countries are concerned. The date at which Turkey will be in a position not to rely on external aid has perpetually moved forward, and it is clear that substantial amounts of project aid will be required for the foreseeable future. On the other hand, the country has enjoyed sensible economic management for most of the period since

January 1980, and Mr Özal's parliamentary majority seems to promise three or four more years of stability. During this period most of the economic aid to Turkey from the West will probably be productively directed, and the climate should be bright for foreign investors. The hope must be that by 1990 the Turkish scene will have been sufficiently transformed to make a return to isolationism and import substitution unthinkable.

There are, however, reasons for worrying that a political change of direction away from the Özal policies could still occur. The major opposition party, Sodep, is committed to *dirigiste* socialist policies and emphasis on the state sector. The right-wing alternative to Mr Özal is the True Path Party. Although the inflationary policies of its predecessor, the Justice Party, ended unfortunately, the JP's economic policies did represent an attempt to please everybody, and many Turks, particularly in the provinces, remember that under those policies they moved from subsistence agriculture into the age of the video recorder. Furthermore, the economic outlook of many army officers remains firmly wedded to the ideas of national defence, state control and reliance on heavy industry. Mr Özal's ideas are not understood by all bureaucrats, and it must be at least disconcerting that his fall from office in July 1982 led to his being replaced by a traditionalist bureaucrat, Mr Adnan Başer Kafaoğlu, who wielded influence at the very highest levels but had little understanding of economic policy. The regression of the Turkish economy during 1983 was slight − growth fell, and exports marked time − but would probably have continued if Mr Özal had not won the November 1983 general elections. There is thus a possibility that economic mismanagement in the medium term could undo some of the success of the past half-decade.

In the longer term, as has already been argued, it seems most likely that Turkey's economy will grow fast over the next few decades and that it will increasingly assert itself as a 'newly industrialized country'. Its international financial importance will therefore be based on strength rather than weakness, and an economically strong country of seventy million inhabitants or more in an area half the size of Europe will undoubtedly play an increasingly independent and powerful role in the Western financial system.

9 Prospects

Turkey's importance to the West

For most of the last hundred years Turkey has been a largely agricultural country straddling two important strategic routes. Its role as a trading nation has been smaller than its size warranted, and until the mass immigration into Western Europe during the 1960s and 1970s it impinged very little on the life of Europe. In this respect there is a clear contrast with Greece — one often pointed out by Turks.

Turkey's main importance to the West is likely to remain its role as a military ally, geographically close to the Soviet Union. Although it may allow bilateral issues (such as the pro-Armenian Congressional Resolution of autumn 1984) to affect the degree of warmth of its relations with NATO, and although it will undoubtedly try to cultivate good diplomatic relations with countries outside the alliance wherever it can, its role as an ally seems unlikely to change. It has few real alternatives to its alliance with the West.

The Turkey of the year 2000, however, will not be the Turkey of 1980, still less that of 1945 or 1919. It is likely to be a country with a population larger than that of any West European nation, well on the way to industrialization and feeling increasingly able to play a strong and independent regional role. If its disputes with Greece, for example, are still continuing, it is likely to have the upper hand, and it is probable that Greece will try to draw as close as possible to Western Europe in response, in an attempt to mobilize Western opinion against its rival.

The increase in Turkey's commercial and economic importance may not be matched by a corresponding acceleration in adopting Western patterns of cultural and daily life, and so the relationship between Western and Turkish public opinions may remain somewhat attenuated.

As with other late-modernizing Mediterranean countries, ethnic Turks will probably appear in most fields of life in Western societies, even in places where the assimilation and social progress of Turkish immigrants has been slow. The probability is, however, that Turkey will be unconsciously semi-isolationist throughout this period and that the political antagonism between government and intellectuals will continue, which will have a negative impact on the country's overall involvement in Western life. None the less, more Turkish film directors, pop musicians, politicians and businessmen will continue to appear in Western societies. The process would be accelerated if the Turkish media fostered, rather than discouraged, assimilation among emigrants, and helped them to be upwardly mobile.

Ironically, an economically and militarily stronger Turkey, one less dependent on aid and able to play a more active regional role, could be a more awkward ally and could possibly prompt a revision of Western perceptions of its military importance. This may be another way of saying that, as Turkey industrializes, it will have to decide how committed it is to the West on grounds of principle as well as on those of short-term self-interest.

This assumes, of course, that Turkey will be able to make up its mind about whether or not it belongs to the West. Despite a very strong sense of national identity and internal solidarity, many Turks seem genuinely uncertain about this. Not long ago the writer heard a Turkish foreign policy analyst discussing in almost agnostic tones whether Turkey was a Balkan country, a Middle Eastern one or a European one. In this context, quite trivial symbolic disputes — a hostile film or television programme — can play a disproportionate part in shaping long-term attitudes. This may change if Turkey becomes a more open and sophisticated society. In the meantime it has few ways of coping with criticism on, for example, human rights issues, because public opinion and public discussion do not operate along quite the same lines as in the West. (It is noticeable, though, that the main current of political opinion in Turkey — that of the centre-right True Path Party, which is relatively immune to censorship and independent — does appear to be able to handle discussion of this sort in a fashion entirely comprehensible in the West.)

Advantages and costs

Closer links with the West would undoubtedly force some readjustments on both sides. It is unlikely that Western public opinion would find it easy to coexist with mass trials of trade unionists, gaoling of journalists and intellectuals, and some of the curbs on civil liberties. In making adjustments on these fronts, Turkey would obviously be preoccupied with the potential for subversion and disorder, and at present any compromise is probably regarded as unacceptable. Clashes of the sort seen at Strasbourg between Turkish and European parliamentarians – and ultimately the press – would thus be likely to increase.

A closer military and economic relationship between the United States and Turkey looks likely to emerge during the next decade and, intrinsically, does not need to be troublesome. The major areas of friction are likely to derive from side-issues raised by Armenian and Greek pressure groups in the United States. The advantages to the USA of a strong ally at the far end of the Mediterranean are obvious. The cost in military aid is not regarded as disproportionate. The US administration is, however, clearly uneasy at the idea of too much bilateralization of its relations with Turkey and will continue to press for improved relations between Western Europe and the Turks.

For Britain – since 1947 not a particularly close partner of Turkey – the relationship is also likely to be reasonably trouble-free, having been confined to gestures of political friendship and increased trade, particularly in defence industries. Early in 1985, a visit to Ankara by the British foreign secretary, Sir Geoffrey Howe, established a warmth of political friendship which had not been seen between the UK and Turkey since 1947.

For most of the countries of mainland Europe the picture is complicated by symbolic or material conflicts. Resolving these – from disputes over rights of migrant workers to disagreements over trade and tariffs – will never be easy while an atmosphere of 'them' and 'us' dominates diplomatic and other contacts. The simplest way forward would probably be to reactivate the Association Agreement and its institutions, within the framework of a reasonably low-profile relationship, without too great expectations on either side. But Turkey's interest in full Community membership at an early date, combined with queries about its own internal situation, raises more profound questions, and probably poses a stumbling-block to any quick, pragmatic breakthrough. It may be that Turkey is pitching its demands too high.

Turkish full membership of the Community would push the frontiers of Europe to the Caucasus and northern Iraq, and would in a sense re-create a political order which has not existed since the Roman Empire. But in the short term Turkey seems to be asking for a warmer and more tolerant political relationship, rather than for economic and political integration of the kind envisaged in the Treaty of Rome. A diplomat-ically successful relationship – for example, one operating through a body like the Council of Europe – would not necessarily have much impact on underlying economic and political realities.

Despite the rapid progress made by Turkey since 1963, its economic and social evolution has not yet gone far enough to make it clear what the country will look like when it is fully urbanized and industrialized. Not everyone, indeed, assumes that those two processes will run their course, although it would be hard to find serious students of Turkish economy and society who predict stagnation or regression. In con-cluding, it is worth looking briefly at the various ways in which Turkish society may develop and the implications of each of these for Turkey's relations with the West.

Possible avenues

(*a*) *The Iberian model.* The most optimistic, and in some ways most likely, prediction one might make is that Turkey is following, a few decades later, the economic and social development of Spain, and that a period of relative authoritarianism will be followed in due course by economic integration with Western Europe and political liberalization. The chief reasons for hesitating about this argument are that Turkey is further from Europe, geographically and culturally, and its disputes with Greece have no real parallel in Spain. In other words, as has been argued above, successful Turkish integration into Europe would call for an act of will, a reaffirmation of national purpose. But in general Turkey's present situation is not unlike that of many European countries (includ-ing of course Germany) which were once considered peripheral or as having doubtful European credentials. Turkey, unlike Spain, however, is not contiguous with Europe, being separated by a belt of East bloc countries.

(*b*) *The Korean model.* The attractions of the economic policies pursued by Far Eastern countries have already been mentioned. Turkish-US relations are much less complex and demanding than those with Western Europe, largely because little interaction with US pressure groups and public opinion is involved. A combination of vigorous economic policies aimed at rapid growth and a strong bilateral relationship with the United States is thus seductive, and, if the 'transition to democracy' meets with difficulties, Turkey's political evolution may well run along these lines for some years to come. Such a bilateral relationship would not, however, any more than it did in the Spanish case, preclude the development of links with Europe some day. The arguments against this scenario seem to be, first, that Turkey and Europe are closely involved with each other, and, second, that the USA, as already mentioned, is not happy about an undiluted bilateral relationship, which could increase political risks inside Turkey and place strains (though probably not very great ones) on US dealings with Western Europe.

(*c*) *The Mexican model.* The two previous models both imply a considerable degree of economic success by Turkey. It is, however, possible to see a slight parallel between Turkey's relationship with Western Europe and that of Mexico and the United States. If foreign investment is stepped up and the expected benefits of industrialization are slow to accrue, Turkey will probably languish on the periphery of Europe, strongly influenced by the continent but with markedly different political characteristics and economically backward. This would probably accelerate the growth of anti-European cultural and political sentiment. Unlike Mexico, Turkey has neighbours outside the Western world to whom it can to some extent turn, and the diplomatic relationship with the West could then be expected to become steadily more difficult. This indeed was the pattern suggested by developments in the 1960s in Turkey, when anti-Western feeling was briefly a serious political and cultural force. Industrial progress was probably the main reason why this disposition waned, though not the only one.

(*d*) *'Swedenization'.* During the late 1970s, supporters of the left-of-centre Republican People's Party flirted with the idea of neutralism along Scandinavian lines. Barring some accident of history — a colossal snub by the United States to Turkey in favour of Greece and a subsequent move out of NATO — such a scenario now seems most unlikely. Turkey will probably have an increasingly active and individualistic foreign policy — for example in the Middle East — and will stress wherever possible that it is not a party to regional conflicts or disputes, but the vogue for Third World attitudes and full-blooded neutralism seems to have passed.

(*e*) *Neo-Ottomanism.* Consciousness of the imperial Ottoman past is a much more politically potent force in Turkey than Islam and, as Turkey regains economic strength, it will be increasingly tempted to assert itself in the Middle East as a leader. At summits of the Islamic Conference, Turkey is beginning to play a more influential role, and this trend may be expected to continue. Since 1923, however, the Turkish Republic has been firmly opposed to irredentism, and although one area (included in the Misak-i Milliye (National Pact) of 1919, which defined Turkey's frontiers after the break-up of the Ottoman Empire) lies outside the boundaries of the Republic, it happens to be in Iraq, a country with which Turkey has good working relations. If Turkey and Europe do find themselves travelling in different directions, regional leadership and the Ottoman/Islamic heritage might well be themes which successive governments would stress. In the foreseeable future, however, Turkey is unlikely to re-emerge as a military power in the Middle East, for instance by sending troops to the Gulf. It is also unlikely, because of the need not to antagonize Congress, to take a more actively anti-Israel line in its foreign policy. But the attraction of playing a strong role as a regional leader is likely to grow, and may prove stronger than that of being a latecomer to Europe. The issue seems to be one which is seriously thought about and argued over by opinion-leaders inside Turkey, even if it is not yet quite formulated in these terms.

(*f*) *Latin American model.* Finally, two variants implying economic and political failure have to be considered. One is that Turkey's social and economic problems will prove insuperable in the long term. If this happened, the country's future would probably be a series of military governments, which would inevitably be isolationist. The dominance of the Turkish armed forces in national life is such that further military involvement in politics is still widely predicted by many Turks (as it is, it must be remembered, by many in Spain and Greece). Nevertheless, Turkey does look set on a dynamic upwards course which makes a picture of economic stagnation less likely, and as the 1980 revolution showed, the gravitational attraction to the West makes it very hard for any military regime in Turkey to regard itself as anything but an interim arrangement.

(g) *Marxism.* The other variant to be considered is a revival of Marxism. The failure of a military regime of the type just described could open the way for a Marxist seizure of power. During the period before the 1980 revolution, a large number of armed Marxist groups had established themselves across the country, but no single group had sufficient support to achieve predominance. There is undoubtedly a considerable following among intellectuals for Marxist ideas, but even allowing for the fact that under present conditions Marxists will not speedily show themselves, it does look as if the experience of the 1970s has somewhat reduced the appeal of Marxism among left-wing Turks. This can be only a matter of surmise. University students are probably still highly radicalized, and so are some parts of the civil service. Support for Soviet communism, however, represents only one version of radicalism, and the appeal of nationalist or neutralist alternatives is considerable. It is unlikely in the short to medium term that Marxism will be permitted to re-emerge in Turkey as a serious political force. Its longer-term potential, as with so many other trends and forces, is linked to Turkey's ability to overcome its social and political problems by successfully industrializing.

Just which of these possible patterns is closest to that which will actually prevail is beyond the scope of this study. Obviously, for as long as Turkey's evolution is basically controlled by the bureaucratic elite described in the early part of this paper, there is likely to be both relative stability and an underlying pro-Western orientation for strategic reasons. However, the West's and Turkey's rulers and publics still know much less about each other than might be expected, and the relationship continues to be complicated by misconceptions and excessive expectations. In the longer term, Turkey's evolution into an industrialized pluralistic society implies a change in the relationship between government and society whose political consequences are likely to be hard to chart but none the less profound for the country's Western allies.

Chronology

1071	Battle of Mantzikert. Turks enter Anatolia.
1326	Ottoman rulers assume the title of Sultan.
1453	Conquest of Istanbul.
1793	Accession of Selim III, first westernizing sultan, later murdered.
1826	Abolition of the Janissaries; beginning of the westernization of the army, diplomacy and education.
1908	Young Turk revolution. End of Ottoman absolutism.
1912	Military coup by Committee of Union and Progress.
1919 -23	War of Independence against allied occupying powers. Mustafa Kemal assumes national leadership. Republic replaces Empire. Ankara becomes capital of Turkey.
1925	Suppression of revolts in eastern Turkey by religious movements. Abolition of the fez and religious costume.
1928	Proclamation of a secular state. Adoption of Latin script.
1930	Greece and Turkey sign peace treaty.
1934	First Five-Year Plan. Establishment of state industries.
1938	Death of Ataturk. Ismet Inonu succeeds as president until 1950.
1946	Opposition Democrat Party established. Beginnings of alliance with the United States.
1948	Turkey joins Organization for European Economic Cooperation (later OECD). Religious education returns to schools after 24 years.
1950	First free elections since establishment of Republic. Democrat Party wins. Celal Bayar becomes president, Adnan Menderes premier.
1958	Devaluation operation ends economic crisis.
1959	Turkey applies for associate membership of EEC.
1960	27 May: military revolution. Menderes and Bayar imprisoned. November: purge of radical officers from junta.
1961	Menderes and two other ex-ministers hanged. New constitution adopted. General elections pr'duce parliamentary deadlock.
1962, 1963	Attempted coups.

1964 President Johnson, in a private letter, warns Turkey not to intervene in Cyprus. Turkey-EEC Agreement goes into force. Süleyman Demirel becomes leader of Justice Party.

1965 Demirel's Justice Party, successor to Democrat Party, wins general elections.

1966 Johnson letter of 1964 published, causing major upsurge of anti-
Americanism. Chief of Staff, Cevdet Sunay, succeeds as president.

1967 Republican People's Party, main opposition, declares itself 'left
of centre'. Renewed crisis in Cyprus.

1969 Justice Party wins elections with 47 per cent of votes.

1970 Divisions in Justice Party. Rival right-wing and Islamic parties
appear.

1971 12 March: army orders Demirel to resign after spate of student
disorders. Curbs on 1961 Constitution follow. Reformist cabinet
of progressive technocrats set up. Parliament continues to
function.

1972 Contest between parliament and military.

1973 Parliament rejects ex-Chief of General Staff as candidate for
presidency. Military withdraw from politics. Surprise victory by
social democratic Republican People's Party in general elections.

1974 Republican People's Party in power in coalition with Islamic
National Salvation Party. General amnesty for political offenders
and criminals.
July–August: military intervention in Cyprus. Ecevit government
resigns, expecting early elections, but these are not held.

1975 After six months' crisis, Demirel forms coalition government
with right-wing nationalist and Islamic partners.

1976 Fierce political contest as 'Nationalist Front coalition' fights off
challenge from social democrats.

1977 June: general elections. Bülent Ecevit's social democratic Republican People's Party falls just short of overall majority.
Right-wing coalition again till December. Economic priorities
ignored.

1978 Ecevit in power with right-wing defectors from Justice Party.
Continuing economic crisis.

1979 Ecevit government rebuffed in mid-term elections. Ecevit resigns
in October, and Demirel forms minority government. Appoints
Turgut Özal head of State Planning Organization.

1980 24 January: Özal unveils radical stabilization programme. Political violence, endemic since 1974, reaching peak levels, with up
to twenty deaths in clashes between extremist groups each day.
12 September: military depose Demirel and proclaim revolution.
Bülend Ulusu becomes prime minister; Özal becomes deputy
prime minister.

1981   Military reduce political violence to trickle, charge former deputy prime minister Alparslan Türkeş with attempt to overthrow constitution by force and armed insurrection. Gaol Ecevit for making criticisms of them in world press. Inflation falls and economic growth resumes for first time for two years. During autumn and winter, private brokers crash.
16 October: pre-coup political parties dissolved. Left-wing trade unionists go on trial.

1982   Arrest of intellectuals in Turkish Peace Association.
August: restrictive new constitution announced.
7 November: constitution approved by 91 per cent in referendum after campaign on its behalf by President Kenan Evren.
June: finance house of 'Banker Kastelli' crashes.
Özal resigns as deputy prime minister on 14 July.

1983   February: new law regulating political parties approved. Party activity resumed from late April. Fifteen new parties formed.
30 May: Grand Turkey Party, successor to pre-coup Justice Party, is banned. Demirel and eighteen politicians exiled. Özal forms Motherland Party. True Path Party replaces Grand Turkey Party.
September: it becomes clear that only three of the fourteen political parties will be allowed to contest elections.
6 November: Özal wins 211 of 400 seats in the general elections. Military-backed Nationalist Democracy Party comes third.

1984   Özal in office, promulgating radical economic reforms. First lifting of martial law in some provinces.

Index

Index

Index

Chatham House Papers

Chatham House Papers provide full and up-to-date information on major issues of foreign policy, together with expert analysis. They are recognized as valuable and authoritative guides to some of the most important policy debates of the day. An annual subscription of six papers costs £22.00. We list current and forthcoming titles overleaf. If you would like to subscribe, please complete the form below.

SUBSCRIPTION ORDER FORM

Please return this form to: or in USA or Canada to:

    Subscriptions,   Subscriptions,
    Routledge & Kegan Paul,   Routledge & Kegan Paul,
    Broadway House,   9 Park Street,
    Newtown Road,   Boston,
    Henley-on-Thames,   MA 02108, USA
    Oxon RG9 1EN, England

Please enter a subscription to Chatham House Papers (£22.00)

I enclose a cheque for _____
Please charge my Access/Barclaycard Number

Signature_____
Name_____
        (BLOCK CAPITALS)

Address _____
_____
_____

Chatham House Papers